W9-BLD-778

OXFORD
STUDENT
PRANKS

OXFORD
STUDENT
PRANKS

A History of
Mischief
& Mayhem

RICHARD O. SMITH

The History Press

For Catherine Wolfe-Smith, Mum and Dad

First published 2010

The History Press
The Mill, Brimscombe Port
Stroud, Gloucestershire, GL5 2QG
www.thehistorypress.co.uk

© Richard O. Smith, 2010

The right of Richard O. Smith to be identified as the Author
of this work has been asserted in accordance with the
Copyrights, Designs and Patents Act 1988.

All rights reserved. No part of this book may be reprinted
or reproduced or utilised in any form or by any electronic,
mechanical or other means, now known or hereafter invented,
including photocopying and recording, or in any information
storage or retrieval system, without the permission in writing
from the Publishers.

British Library Cataloguing in Publication Data.
A catalogue record for this book is available from the British Library.

ISBN 978 0 7524 5650 8

Typesetting and origination by The History Press
Printed in Great Britain

CONTENTS

Oxford students. Courtesy of the *Oxford Mail/Oxford Times* (Newsquest Oxfordshire)

INTRODUCTION

B efore you start to read this book, let's play a quick game of word association. Oh go on, it'll be fun. OK, I'll start: 'student'. Now you say a word ...

Right, I'm guessing you said one, or more likely several, of the following words: dossers, drunk, lazy, drugs, over-sexed, alcohol, annoying, boozy, loud, privileged, traffic cones.

If you said any of the following words: debt, deadline, stress, tutorial, anxiety, lectures, intensive, poverty, pressure, fees, essay ... then you're (a) probably far closer to the truth than the first group and (b) almost certainly a student yourself.

If you uttered words from the first group, then you're probably a townsperson. It isn't necessarily mandatory to have originated from Oxford to be a townsperson; just doggedly possessing prejudice against students – or, to give them their full name: bloody students – will suffice for 'Town' status (as opposed to 'Gown', who are Oxford University and their students).

Students, of course, spend their time and money perennially stocking up on supermarket own-brand cider, rolling Rizla papers (giant size) and recording the *Neighbours* repeat (because it's on at 1 p.m. and that's far too early to expect them to be up). Other favoured activities include throwing-up near kebab vans, moving diversion signs, rolling spliffs of equivalent size to be mistaken for stock at a carpet warehouse, arranging to meet a fellow student 'first thing tomorrow morning' (i.e. noon) and placing impromptu traffic cone hats on any civic statues that the council has carelessly left outside on public display. Oh yes, and they also dedicate a lot of time and sweaty energy to giving each other chlamydia.

This is an accurate portrayal of the Oxford student. Or rather, it's an inaccurate myth re-painted as reality.

Student behaviour does seem to permeate deeply into the public's understanding of Oxford, and, for all the defined separateness that both Town and Gown have been indefatigably engaged in establishing throughout the centuries, there still exists a lazy one-size-fits-all perception of an Oxford inhabitant. Frequently, whenever I reveal that I'm an Oxonian, the encountered default response is similar to 'you must be posh'. Often the visitor's reference point for the city is *Brideshead Revisited*. Indeed, you almost encounter the belief that Oxford's so posh we've probably got a Kentucky Fried Grouse in Cornmarket.

Not that this perceived aloofness isn't entirely without a justified source. The Queen's College statutes, composed in the fourteenth century, made official provision for corporal punishment, but 'only for the poor boys'. Brasenose, Christ Church and Corpus Christi all provided beatings for any student up to the age of twenty, with a birching administered for anyone caught conversing in English rather than Latin. (Oddly, this became an advertised fact, viewed as attracting students to their colleges, paid for by parents who approved of such discipline.)

However, the ancient glacier that is the source of this river of privilege is quickly melting and, not unlike the real, non-metaphorical glaciers, the suddenly increased rate of thawing has happened in relatively recent times, after standing frozen and unchanged for centuries.

For the the last few decades, unlike the last few centuries, Oxford has no longer been the almost exclusive preserve of upper middle-class families. Oxford is painfully aware of its requirement to become a meritocracy. The old 'I remember your father' college system of merely awarding places is now, mercifully, obsolete. But the public's perception isn't quite yet prepared to join it in becoming obsolete.

So do students behave worse these days? Well, let's have a quick look at how they behaved in the past ...

Oxford's skyline.

In 1301 Nicholas de Marche broke into a fellow student's house and stabbed scholar Thomas Horncastle. The next day Thomas Horncastle violently assaulted de Marche in Schools Street. Spotting the altercation, another student intervened and was murdered by a sword-brandishing de Marche, his blood-strewn corpse abandoned in Catte Street.

Even respectable townspeople in trade could expect similar appalling treatment from students. John Crosby, a fifteenth-century student at Lincoln College, entered a glove-maker's shop in Cornmarket and, upon learning that there was a slight delay in the gloves' production, attempted to stab the glove maker to death (well, if you allow standards to slip …).

Not that history records the townspeople behaving much better. Richard Hawkins, a boatman based at Fisher Row on Oxford's canal, astounded shoppers in Oxford's Covered Market in 1789 when he offered his wife for sale by public auction. William Gibbs, a stonemason in Oxford working on repairs to the castle, purchased her for five shillings!

The behaviour of the Oxford University officials also left a lot to be desired when female students finally arrived at Oxford in the late nineteenth century. One female undergraduate was moved to fulminate in the 1980s: 'it's the story of the hemispheres in our skulls, not our shirts, that matters'. One British tabloid picked up the story and felt an obligation to point out that in this context hemispheres were not 'bouncy breasts' (which they helpfully illustrated with a photo of some pendulous breasts alongside a diagrammatic north and south hemisphere – ignoring the callous reality that the destiny of all hemispheres is to eventually go south).

Official Oxford University advice to female students in the inter-war years was to 'avoid running away from male undergraduates and townsmen, as men are aroused by the spirit of the chase'. Still, it's somehow reassuring that the University authorities harboured an equally low view of men as they did women. Magdalen College, the last of the Oxford colleges to refuse to deliver a lecture if a woman was present, finally permitted females into its lecture halls in 1906, though not into their college until 1979.

If the townspeople and formerly chauvinistic colleges behave better nowadays, then the students certainly do too – although some modern-day freshers undoubtedly receive a culture shock after checking out of Hotel Parents. Two University College students in the early 1990s suffered the rare indignity of scouts refusing to clean their room (if you're unfamiliar with Oxford parlance, then I should point out that a 'scout' is a college cleaner). Unwashed plates, stained with congealed leftovers, were poorly hidden under rugs and settee cushions – basically it was an unfit environment to keep pigs; and if they had, the RSPCA would have been forced to remove them.

And yet, unclean rooms and mild annoyances aside, Oxford students have behaved unimaginably worse in times gone by than they do today. If you've ever tutted at students blocking the pavement or carrying on a conversation around you whilst seemingly oblivious to your presence (students please note: simply orating 'I was so drunk last night' does not, in itself, constitute an anecdote), then you should read on to compare how splendidly students behave themselves now.

Richard O. Smith, 2010

A pensive gargoyle.

ONE

THE THIRTEENTH CENTURY

Although Oxford chooses to shrug off its Town and Gown divisions whenever inspected from outside (like an arguing couple who claim their spats are an inevitable part of a deeper relationship that disqualifies outsiders from understanding or advising) and the city projects an unwavering party line of unity within a shared municipal identity, rivalry between the Town and Gown has been present from the University's inception.

The Gown's ascendancy over the Town was practically secured as early as 1214 by the papal legate, and continued to become more concentrated over each passing decade. The townspeople would frequently retaliate. Some of their more moderate tactics included creating huge rubbish piles directly outside college gates and slaughtering livestock in the street, next to a college building and deliberately underneath a (preferably opened) scholar's window.

CARDINAL SIN

Such was the extent of student debauchery in Oxford that word eventually reached the Vatican. A papal legate was despatched to Oxford in an attempt to sanctify the city and save its collective soul. Unsurprisingly, matters did not follow the papal plan.

Corruption reform was intended to start at Osney Abbey, where the papal legate was to reside during his stay in Oxford, and the chosen location for his first reforming speech. Oxford's scholarly population hatched a plan that was so cunning it would have scored a ten on the Baldrick plan scale of cunning; equally it would have scored a ten on the Baldrick plan scale of ineptitude.

The plan was: visit the cardinal daily and ply him with copious plates of food, bottles of strong wine, port and beer … and a working girl. The students were putting all their eggs in one fraying basket i.e. the entire plan pivoted on the certainty that he would be a bent papal legate. Unfortunately for the entire plan, he wasn't. Therefore it was time for Plan B; regrettably, Plan B would also have been approved by Baldrick.

Plan B involved a sizable student army marching to Osney Abbey to engage in a mutually respectful two-way dialogue/kick his holy ass back to Rome. Sensing the students' intentions were not peaceful, the gatemen at Osney Abbey refused the scholars entry. Tensions were escalated by several of the legate's entourage shouting Italian-accented insults at the Oxford scholars from atop the abbey walls (this is getting so *Monty Python* …).

Sparked into even greater anger by the Italian taunters, the scholar army then busied themselves collecting fallen tree trunks to provide makeshift battering rams and improvised weapons. The ecclesiastical Italians similarly tooled themselves up with staves, pikes and homemade spears – similar to what one imagines the paramilitary wing of the Salvation Army would be like.

As dusk descended, the students initiated their attack. The Osney cook, who was the brother of the papal legate, had clearly studied Module One of Tactics for Defending a Medieval Castle: The Boiling Pot. Predicting the attempted student invasion of the abbey, he utilised the available time during the siege whilst the scholars were arboretum-bound collecting weapons, to order everyone to boil bowls of water or oil. As soon as the students broke through the abbey gates, he provided the prior agreed signal for the boiling liquids to cascade down onto the students below. A Welsh student was badly scolded in the face and retaliated by firing an arrow at the cook, killing him instantly.

Sensing they were outnumbered, the cardinal then raised the order for his entourage to abandon the main abbey buildings, but take refuge in the belfry. Shortly after midnight, the besieged papal delegation decided to relay a message outlining their predicament to attract help. Yet accomplishing this objective would necessitate sending a man out past the amassed students. Hence a distraction for the students was duly planned. (If only they'd had some traffic cones to put out … students are undeniably incapable of not being distracted by traffic cones.)

Fortunately for the besieged cardinal, students possess a hardwired inability to avoid alcohol too – and there were bountiful amounts in the abbey resulting form the donations/attempted bribes. Thus, as the student voices became louder as the night wore on the cardinal was elected as the man to attempt an escape, tiptoeing out of the abbey, past the drunken and loudly loquacious students, to reach the authorities grasping a written proclamation for support and reinforcements.

Using the moonlight reflected from the River Thames, the cardinal was able to escape (well, a man dressed head to foot in a bright red velvet gown accessorized with a huge red shiny hat isn't going to be that easy to spot), whilst the boozy students were presumably too enraptured by their own conversations to notice an escapee cardinal.

The cardinal headed south along the Thames path, reaching Abingdon before dawn. Here he received word that the King was currently (and somewhat fortuitously for the cardinal) staying in nearby Wallingford. Upon hearing the cardinal's account of the Osney Abbey events, the King's mood quickly turned bellicose and an army, led by a royal standard bearer, was hastily despatched from the Wallingford barracks to Oxford. The professional army soon reached Osney and stormed virtually unopposed through the abbey gates, leaving the huddled and newly meek students to ponder their ironic fate of now being the besieged as opposed to the besieger of only thirty-six hours earlier.

Justice was swift and pernicious, and thirty-eight students were rounded up and sent to Wallingford to face the King. From here, they journeyed by open-top carts – their humiliation was deliberate – to London, where a delegation of high-ranking bishops intervened, eventually brokering their absolution from the legate, but only after sufficient penance had been pledged to serve as a visible punishment.

The legate may have eventually won the battle, but the war on Oxford's immorality would not prove so accomplishable; there's certainly been no sign of a breakthrough in the ensuing 800 years!

CAMBRIDGE'S INSALUBRIOUS ORIGINS

Oxford's students already had form when it came to papal legates, as a townswoman (supposedly a prostitute) was killed by two students in 1209. Enraged townspeople stormed the students' house, and, finding them out, the mob opted to kill several innocent students instead who had the misfortune to share dwellings. Fearing similar recriminations, the actual murderers considered it expedient to flee Oxford instantaneously. Once they had journeyed approximately ninety miles east, they decided it would be safe to remain there, and form their own University. That, ladies and gentleman, is how Cambridge University was founded in 1209: by two Oxford rejects who were prostitute murderers. How do you feel now, Cambridge?

As a consequence of the townspeople murdering students (not, you notice, the townswoman being slain), a papal bull was issued banning all teaching in Oxford for several months.

MACE IN YOUR FACE

Such was the deteriorating relationship between Oxford University and the townspeople, that as early as 1242 an official bailiff had been appointed, charged with the specific responsibility of keeping order between a skirmishing Town and Gown. The first holder of this newly minted bailiff's badge was Peter Torald, who had previously been the city's sheriff in 1225, and, although he encountered elements encumbering the peace process, he evidently performed the role with sufficient success to be subsequently twice elected as mayor.

In the thirteenth century, Oxford hosted numerous city riots that an average football hooligan would have considered unnecessarily violent and pointlessly irresponsible. On 21 February 1298, the town's bailiff was parading through the city, proudly holding the heraldic mace of office. On reaching Carfax, he discovered a mob loitering outside St Martin's Church (the tower still survives today, albeit rechristened Carfax Tower). The mob were students and, in some thirteenth-century equivalent of flash mobbing, had all agreed to convene at Carfax at this appointed time, with the intention of stealing the bailiff's mace – which is such a defining student prank.

The bailiff was one Robert Worminghall, who had been elected to the role fully eight years earlier, in what I'm sure was a fair and transparent election, and utterly disconnected to the fact that his brother Phillip Worminghall was the mayor and subsequently in charge of appointing the well-remunerated post.

There are only so many students that one man can hit over the head with a sturdy and now evidently dented – mace, and an immense discrepancy in personnel quickly occurred in the students' favour (contemporary accounts conferred that the students were too many to comfortably count though with medieval peasants commonly innumerate, this doesn't help much), whilst the bailiff was left 'with a mere handful of townspeople'. Snatching the mace, the students then committed a tactical mistake. Rather than heading back to their college bars with the mace held aloft like a captured sports trophy, they decided to remain at Carfax and await a retaliatory mob of townspeople galvanised into revenge by the circulating news.

Ringing the bells of St Martin's summoned town reinforcement and swelled their side to an intimidating majority over the students. Several students were then attacked, with bottles being broken over heads like a big-budget Western salon fight scene. The perceived leader of the students was captured and marched towards the town jail. Just as a lengthy stay in the stocks looked likely as a plausible excuse for missing a tutorial, a further group of student reinforcements arrived, which reclaimed the personnel majority back in favour of the Gown.

Radcliffe Square –
spot the traffic cone!

Having sprung the student ringleader from jail, the angry student
mob now marched towards the bailiff's house. They smashed down
the doors and windows of his abode, like a particularly angry, big bad
wolf (the house was made of timber, not brick – the bailiff clearly didn't
read fairytales), and proceeded to demolish the dwelling. Next the
students unsheathed their swords and advised the bailiff to offer his last
prayer to God, whom he was due to meet imminently.

With a critical sense of timing almost non-existence outside drama
productions, reinforcements of townspeople arrived and re-engaged
with the students, allowing the bailiff to escape and hide in a house built
on the site now occupied by Radcliffe Square.

So, after his escape, could peace finally descend on the city again?
No, in fact, far from being over, an escalation in the crisis was about
to happen. The next day, students arrived in the morning at St Mary's
Church in the High Street (being students, I'm guessing it wasn't
that early: they probably said 'meet at 11 a.m.', with the first student
eventually showing up at noon-ish). Ignoring the protocol of a church
providing sanctuary, they entered the building and 'beat wickedly and
trampled thereon those inside'.

When Thomas Attechurcheye, a local tradesman, left his house to
walk the two miles into Oxford from the neighbouring village of Iffley
that morning, he probably wasn't expecting a deviation from his normal

St Mary's Church (right) and the Radcliffe Camera.

commuting routine. Unfortunately, he was never to return home, as his journey along the High Street took him past St Mary's Church and straight into the eye of a riotous storm. Identified as a member of the trading classes by his clothes, the students realised that Thomas was a townsman, and promptly murdered the unfortunate local. Unsettled by the violent escalation, several townspeople began to disperse and sought sanctuary inside other city churches.

Spotting the town burgess John Dorre, who had presumably felt obligated not to join the retreat given his official standing, the students forcibly dragged him by his hair until they were level with the altar inside St Mary's, before kicking him unconscious. The scholars then turned to the frightened congregation and issued a proclamation to the fearful townspeople inside that they would soon all be robbed and murdered. Such rebarbative statements ensured the townspeople instantly fled through all available (and unavailable, in the case of much window breaking) exits.

Two days later, the battle was re-ignited. Indeed, this time it had escalated to nuclear. Fully 1,000 students, armed with bows and full quivers, pikes and swords, broke into the houses of Oxford residents at dinner time, in an entirely pre-planned operation. Four workplaces were identified as strategic targets in the town: a butcher's shop, spice emporium, cutlery store and restaurant. The students stole every item they could carry and took the assembled swag to their colleges, whilst simultaneously committing vandalism on a scale that would have amply outraged the average bus-stop-vandalising, delinquent teenage hoodie.

This sufficiently incensed the town's people to seek murderous revenge, and a student was duly chased, cornered and killed; his body was left face down in the street as a symbol to the impunity of scholarly privileges.

Both brothers, Robert and Philip Worminghall, serving as bailiff and mayor respectively, were exiled from Oxford as a punitive gesture for their active role in the rioting, and specifically for allowing a student to be murdered on what was deemed to be their watch. Notice how blame was purely apportioned to the Town side – a rumbling injustice that would continue to cause friction throughout the centuries ahead.

Yet, with fatal causalities on both the Town and Gown sides, neither party was ready to endorse appeasement. The following year, the townspeople, their anger clearly still smouldering, defiantly elected Robert as mayor for another term – this was despite him having been banished from Oxford for several months for his role in murdering a student and injuring several others – which might constitute a slightly embarrassing scandal in today's media-savvy age (indeed, both Worminghall brothers had so many skeletons in their cupboard that they could hardly shut the door). Presumably Robert campaigned on a 'reduce Oxford's congestion, kill a student' ticket.

Re-electing him as mayor was not an expedient move by the town, as it led indirectly to an additional tightening of University privileges over the city, decreed by royal assent. Almost inevitably, this led to further shock waves of discontent amongst the townspeople: gunpowder was being stored, and sparks were about to fly.

RUFFIAN TREATMENT

Henry III branded Oxford students 'incorrigible and rebellious ruffians' and ordered every student to register, or as he said at the time: 'to matricula' (the origins of matriculation derives from the word 'matriculate' – literally meaning 'registration roll'). By formally joining the University on a Saturday at the beginning of Michaelmas term when Oxford's new student intake matriculate, the ceremony continues to indulge Henry III's branding of the aforementioned incorrigible and rebellious ruffians – aka students.

FORWARD ESCORTS

The University's expanding authority inevitably caused jealous frictions with the townspeople, particularly as the colleges enjoyed privileges set by the King. Although the university attempted to control Oxford as if they were the sole inhabitants of the town, Oxford was growing in size outside the University, as proved by an inventory of buildings conducted in 1279, which listed 466 houses, 147 shops and 48 taverns. Nowadays, the numbers would be 466 houses in Oxford (that are not sub-let), 147 mobile phone shops and 48 coffee shops.

The perceived image of the townspeople focused almost entirely on their ability to provide menial support work for the University. Inevitably, this led to multiple conflicts, very much of the bloody variety. Especially given that an expansive employment sector for the townspeople was prostitution, whose scale had become sufficiently notorious for news to have reached the Pope; the pontiff once again despatching a communiqué to Oxford's students warning of 'debauch behaviour'.

The University decided to curtail student debauchery by exiling prostitutes from Oxford; a directive somewhat half-heartedly implemented by the Town. John Ayliffe states in *The Ancient and Present State of the University of Oxford* that, 'King Henry III ordered the town mayor and bailiffs to release all lewd women then in prison, on condition that they leave the town immediately, declaring that they do not come to Oxford again. Upon publication of this writ many loose women were expelled from Oxford.' So, around the 1230s, Oxford provided an amnesty for its sex workers, a policy overseen by the city's mayor, Adam Fettiplace. Fettiplace was a rich merchant, owning both the impressively capacious Drapery Hall in Cornmarket and Shelde Hall located near St Edmund Hall; it's probably a fair assumption that Fettiplace was mixing both business and pleasure with this encouraging legislation that inevitably attracted more prostitutes to the city given that a free ride home was a preferable choice to the customary jail sentence provided elsewhere by rival towns.

This missive of publicised expulsion may well have been spin. A traveller entering Oxford at the time would not have had to seek prostitutes, as they would almost certainly have found him, since the large client base of rich and morally duplicitous students ensured Oxford attracted huge harlot numbers, many of whom were tolerated characters around the town and not shy in advancing their offered services to students. Of course, there were not many other employment opportunities for females requiring paid work at the time; a visit to a thirteenth-century careers adviser would have been frustratingly unproductive.

SIMON SAYS

Oxford University owes its continued existence to the rebellious nature of its students. In 1263 Henry III ordered that Oxford University should close and all the scholars migrate to Northampton, decreed as the site of a new university.

This was the direct result of an early attempt at a written constitution being taken exceptionally badly by the ruling monarch, who chose to view it as a threat to his regal omnipotence. Several prominent barons, led by Simon de Montford, had authored a document entitled *Provisions of Oxford* that proposed a system of parliamentary rule comprised of twenty-four delegates: twelve elected by the barons and twelve by the King. This embryonic attempt at democracy, resulting in arguably the country's first written constitution, sparked the Second Baron's War – an early English civil war.

Oxford viewed the baronial cause as progressive, and supported it loudly. Henry III therefore decided, like all textbook tyrants, to close down the University – even summoning his knights to Oxford to intimidate students. He then issued a decree that Oxford's entire student population should leave the city *en masse* and reconvene in Northampton.

Thankfully, only a few took heed of this royal directive and most students rebelled by staying put in Oxford (if only the mass migratory march to Northampton hadn't been timetabled to leave so early in the morning). Presumably, such rebellious behaviour saving Oxford University would have rendered that generation of students unbearable afterwards: 'You need to be at the lecture for 9 a.m. sharp, and hand in your completed essay then too'. 'No way, I'm going to have a lie-in until 11 a.m. and I'm not doing any essays – remember how the entire future of Oxford University depended on me refusing to do what I'm told?!'

IMPISH BEHAVIOUR

In 1290 a delegation of townspeople appealed to parliament, requesting that the choking oppression of the University's authority over the town should be diluted. Parliament's response was merely to increase the discrepancy between privileges experienced by Town and Gown, going so far as to reassert the University's authority to judge any crime involving students – with two exceptions: murder and mayhem. Since the two most popular student past times at the time were murder and mayhem, this did at least allow for some judicial town authority – until even this right was seized back by the University when they negated the two exemption clauses.

After yet another Town and Gown riot in 1298, the Bishop of Lincoln personally intervened (Oxford was then partly within the diocese of Lincoln). He blamed the Town side completely for all the rioting, injuries and damage, and helpfully recommended extra penance for the townspeople to endure.

OXFORD LINCS

Insidious practices abounded in the formative years of the University. Colleges would install their members as parish priests and then claim the vicarage, or in some cases even the parish, as college property. In 1286 a Merton student attempted to occupy a parish church whilst the funeral for the previous vicar was being conducted. This led to a mass brawl between the pews, which saw the Oxford University delegation beaten back with sickles and billhooks.

At another parish church in Lincolnshire in 1302, Merton's representatives were again chased away by an angry armed mob after a scholar had attempted to interrupt the vicar during evening song to read aloud from the pulpit an alleged letter from the Pope proclaiming Merton's ownership of the parish and allowing the assembled congregation an hour to vacate the premises. Nice try.

Proof of Oxford's bellicose leanings during this age is shown in Merton's archives, which records that a special sword allowance was made for their proctors.

BACON FRIAR

Cambridge University was founded in 1209. By 1210 Oxford was probably well established at organising student pranks against Cambridge. Certainly within forty years of Fenland Polytechnic's origination, Oxford students were victimising their Cambridge counterparts with highly organised tomfoolery. The early thirteenth-century scholar and pioneering advocate of the experimental method, Roger Bacon, was responsible for the eponymous folly that still provides Folly Bridge with its name today, and was so significant in Oxford University's formative decades that he revelled in the adopted nicknamed Doctor Mirabilis. Evidently one inhabits a posh place when the nicknames handed out are in Latin. Doctor Mirabilis – should you have blind spots in your Latin vocabulary as large as mine – translates as 'wonderful teacher'.

After having likely come up to Oxford at the age of thirteen (given how cruelly truncated life expectancy was in the thirteenth century, adult life was compelled to start earlier), Bacon later invited a delegation of Cambridge University fellows and students to visit Oxford. Bacon recruited the finest Oxford minds from the University, even holding auditions to ensure he hired the desired academic dream team, and fitted those who had earned a successful call-back with peasant clothes; he even smeared dirt to capture that authentic just-been-wrestling-a-wild-boar look that was so fashionably *de rigour* throughout those early medieval years. Bacon then schooled his mock peasant ensemble in deceiving accents to appear illiterate and uneducated.

Make no mistake about it – this was clearly a thirteenth-century student prank with a budget; there are Hollywood movies starring Julia Roberts and Brad Pitt that got made with smaller budgets than this project received.

Bacon insisted that the majority of his Oxford 'peasants' were routinely tri-lingual, conversant in Latin and Greek as well as their native tongue. And as student pranks go as feats of scale and imaginative, it sure beats unscrewing the top of a salt cellar prior to passing it at dinner.

Bacon initiated and undertook the entire project to ensure that when a Cambridge University delegation encountered the troupe of Oxford 'peasants', they conversed in Greek and Latin to discuss the works of Aristotle. This, Bacon believed, proved to Cambridge that Oxford was so immeasurably superior, even the local peasants were schooled in the classics and effortlessly tri-lingual.

Opus Majus, written by Bacon in the mid-thirteenth century, came in just short of 900 pages: *Opus Majus* translates, fittingly enough, as Major Work. Whereas most books ultimately fail to live up to their titles (e.g. no mockingbirds appear, let alone get killed, in Harper Lee's epic) *Opus Majus* truly does both deserve, and live up to, its bar-raising title. Mixing philosophy, astronomy, religious criticism and medical anatomy, the work also speculates that the future will include ships powered by steam. Bacon discovered refraction in light, the convex lens and was also a pioneering horologist and philologist, designed propellers for boats and proposed the reasoning behind shooting stars (proved correct centuries later).

After the Franciscans had arrived in Oxford in 1224 and established Greyfriars, Bacon obtained the crucial support of Oxford's first Chancellor and was allowed to introduce the subject of mathematics to the University. He also developed a pioneering magnifying glass and researched proof that the earth was round – also hypothesised in *Opus Majus*.

The book implores the reader to be receptive towards evidence-based scientific observation, and speculates that the earth and planets revolve around the sun and not vice versa (just a mere 300 years before Polish monk Nicolaus Copernicus and 400 years ahead of Galileo). Needless to say, given the decidedly stronger than straight-to-bed-and-no-supper punishment that Copernicus and Galileo received for advancing such perceived anti-religious dogma 300 years later, the ruling Catholic Church considered it their duty to ensure that they had his …well … Bacon.

If you were a practising monk in the thirteenth century (and Bacon had taken Catholic religious orders as a Franciscan) prior to producing a book appertaining to provide scientific proof destroying the hitherto universally adopted Biblical truism that the earth was created by God as the centre of the universe, then you have to expect that detail to come up at your workplace annual appraisal. As a result, Bacon was placed under permanent house arrest in a folly tower in Oxford.

In a fitting monument, appropriately reverential towards this pioneering scholar of global importance, a philosopher who germinated European empiricalism, Bacon is commemorated in Oxford by a … errr …ahem … concrete slab breeze-blocked to the wall of the Westgate car park, behind a tree renowned for being carpeted with dog mess. Anyone else suspect a Cambridge-based architect was behind the monument's design? Probably best to remember him by Folly Bridge being so named.

TWO

THE FOURTEENTH CENTURY

As if medieval Oxford didn't provide sufficient danger lurking outside the college walls, fourteenth-century students also discovered there was a permanent threat to their wellbeing from other students inside the colleges just as brutal as the violent aspirations of the townspeople. Bizarrely, Oxford students tended to group themselves into divergent tribes representative of their geological origins. Such tribal divaricating was accentuated by the then custom of colleges catering purely for students from one given location – an unchallenged tradition that continued, albeit in diluted form, until well into the twentieth century. Hence St Edmund Hall has associations with the South West, New College with Winchester, Trinity with the North East, Jesus with Wales, etc.

The Welsh occupied the role of both bully and victim in Oxford's early academic history. However, it was another regional grouping of students, the Irish, who caused the University to react to a particularly ferocious ambush on scholars from northern England, to legislate that all Oxford students must reside in halls and no longer in lodgings with townspeople. This unquestionably added to the sense of separation between Town and Gown.

If you associate educational establishments with suffering gang culture, then you're probably thinking of inner city schools in areas attempting to shrug off social deprivation. In fact, gang culture was epidemic amongst Oxford University students from the fourteenth century onwards. Five principal gangs existed amongst the student population of medieval Oxford University, and membership was common, bordering on *de rigour*. Never underestimate the power of nationalism, as the gangs were recruited and identified along strictly geographical lines. Gangs were known as, and recruited from, the Scots, Welsh, Irish, northern and southern English. Paradoxically, the strongest 'national' rivalry was between the northern and southern English gangs.

Enter the proctors, who are the University's own prefects charged with maintaining law and order throughout the centuries. They were initially recruited by the medieval university with strict geographical sectarianism: proctors were appointed with 50 per cent from both northern and southern England, to placate regional partisanship. Proctors held an extremely powerful office, with considerably exaggerated powers to those they enjoy today: in the fourteenth century they were not only concerned with discipline and administering fines to unruly students, but could actively veto University policy. They were also armed with arquebuses. But the proctors' manpower was repeatedly shown as inadequate when it came to the force of student rioting. And there were no students more ferocious than the Welsh. In 1303 student William de Roule was murdered by Welsh students after being found guilty of committing the crime of not being Welsh. The Welsh students issued several bilious statements, vowing revenge on other students for 'provocation' ('provocation' in this context meant 'not originating from Wales').

A large-scaled, pre-arranged fight duly occurred between the Welsh and other student groups in a field outside of Oxford. Anthony Wood, although writing in the seventeenth century, informs us that all sides had banners and flags as they marched into battle.

The northern England gang joined forces with the Welsh, and thereby proved to be an undefeatable majority, destroying the Scots, Irish and southern English. Then, showing the inherent treachery amongst the student gangs, the northern English turned on the Welsh. Wood graphically describes how the northern scholars led the Welshmen to the gates:

… causing them first to piss on them, and then to kiss the place on which they had pissed. But being not content with that, they then said Welshmen stooped to kiss it, would knock their heads against the gates in such an inhuman manner, and they would force blood out of the noses of some, and tears from the eyes of others.

So it's official then – northerners were the hardest students. Well done. And everyone went home without a degree.

Such was the seriousness of the battles that the King became involved, prompting the students to hastily raise 700 marks, 400 of which they offered to the King in anticipation of purchasing royal appeasement, with the other 300 marks being obsequiously handed to his son Edward in order to avoid later retribution should he inherit the throne.

WELSH RARE BIT: SPEESE TOASTED

Revenge was sought against the Welsh students, who were blamed for starting the tribal battles. In 1343 Richard de Langeleghe murdered a Welsh student with a bodkin (a piercing instrument used to make holes in cloth). Richard Gille knifed John Martyn to death inside Queen's College and, in the same year, student John Kirkeby arranged a campaign of targeted burglaries and street robbing, and then an organised riot, against the Welsh students.

After the heated situation had bubbled for several decades – with sudden intermittent geezer-blows of conflict erupting every few years – battle commenced again in the fourth week of Hilary Term in 1389.

Thomas Chaplain Speese and John Kirkby recruited and led a rabble student army whose pronounced aim was to rid Oxford of Welsh students. They planned an anti-Welsh pogrom in Oxford, and toasted their army with a battle cry of 'war, war, war, sle, sle, sle the Walsh doggyes and her whelyps' ('whelyps' being an Old English word of Saxon and Dutch derivation for 'puppy').

Proceeding to terrorise the streets of Oxford, Speese and Kirby's student army chanted and daubed their slogan: 'and whoso loketh out of his howese, he shalle in good soute be dead, the walsh doggyes and her whelyps'. Their battle cry and sloganeering enables a contemporary bystander to deduce that: (a) this was a pre-meditated and assiduously planned operation (b) their battle cry was far too reliant on canine-based insults (c) they forget to run their slogan through the Windows spellchecker facility.

RUNNING WITH THE BULLS

Prostitution, coupled with the other traditional Oxford recreational activity enjoyed by both townspeople and students (i.e. rioting), led directly to the next battle. Only this time Oxford students appeared to have forgotten the importance of the Pope's religion. Oxford had been used to staging parochial battles between its own population, and student pitted against different geographically zoned student, but now the town decided it was ready to take on international competition: namely Rome.

Pope Boniface IX (no, that's his real name) issued a bull in 1395 enshrining authoritative rights to English bishops. Ruling monarch Richard II objected strongly, interpreting this as a calculated attempt to reduce his power and refused to acknowledge the bull. However, Oxford publicly supported the Pope, resulting in Richard II despatching a bishop to Oxford to remind the citizens of their supposed dutiful loyalty to their monarch. On hearing of the bishop's arrival through the Westgate, students immediately barricaded the entrance to St Mary's Church, and stood guard to block his entry. Unable to address the congregation and assembled Church leaders within, the bishop and his entourage merely turned their horses around and fled Oxford. Dismantling the barricades outside St Mary's, the students were evidently disappointed that the afternoon's expected riot had not materialised. Therefore they started, with some alacrity, their own riot amongst themselves, engaging in a bloody battle between the students of northern and southern origin.

Richard III had won the argument, and the papal legate of 1395 was not adopted by Oxford, though it's debateable if anyone noticed given the on going riot focusing the city's attention.

Town and Gown riot. (© Images & Voices, Oxfordshire County Council)

ST SCHOLASTICA'S DAY MASSACRE

Student japes are one way of annoying the townspeople that has remained remarkably consistent over the ensuing centuries: students throwing flour, eggs and cat food over each other after sitting their Finals carelessly catching unfortunate locals and tourists in their crossfire, and the university now routinely despatches proctors to stand guard in strategically identified egging areas. Although technically empowered to remove degrees, this rarely occurs in practice – which risks the townspeople resurrecting the spirit of 1355.

Although the St Scholastica's Day Massacre still obtains the headlines for the ultimate Town v. Gown riot, it was by no means the first. It may have been the most deadly, yet, far from being a trailblazing event, such a descent into mindless city-wide rioting was becoming genuinely passé by 1355.

Whereas nowadays seemingly the only people capable of remembering just one Saint's Day are a handful of middle-Englanders desperate for resurrected acknowledgement of our national St George (who was actually Turkish, but hey), saints' days were familiar and acknowledged throughout medieval England's feudal class system.

An abiding reason for a peasant's knowledge, affection and allegiance to the various saints' days in the calendar was principally because they were deemed workers' holidays. Medieval workers could claim nearly eighty days of annual leave entitlement. Hence saints' days were associated with fighting students, since there wasn't much else to do in medieval Oxford on a day off apart from drinking, fighting, visiting church and/or prostitutes or staying in to die of the plague.

Both students and Oxford citizens would continue to die in street battles well into the Victorian era, but the death toll was never higher than on 10 and 11 February 1355.

Walter Springeheuse and Roger Chesterfield were, un-characteristically for modern students, both ordained priests. They were also, characteristically for modern students, both drinking heavily in a public house. Lacking elementary negotiation skills, they complained about the quality of their drinks (some accounts state ale, others wine – so it was probably both, in an extra large glass) by throwing them in the face of the landlord of the tavern they were frequenting: The Swyndlstock Tavern – now disappointingly a bank at Carfax.

This led directly to the mother of all bar fights, and college chapel bells were rung to summon student reinforcements, while town peals tolled to recruit Oxonians to the battle.

The University Chancellor was briefed by one of his advisers – in possibly the worse example of public figure advising since President J.F.

Kennedy's advisers suggested he drive through Dallas in an open-top car – that a guaranteed method of curtailing the rioting would be to appear in full Chancellor's robes and regalia to remind the townspeople and students of the Chancellor's authority. The Chancellor duly arrived in full ceremonial robes, immediately received several rocks to the head and body, and ran away screaming to the sanctuary of his rooms.

Meanwhile, the sound of bells and sight of rising smoke had alerted the citizens of Abingdon, who marched towards Oxford. The town militia, in charge of manning Oxford's southern gate, perceptively evaluated from body language that their intentions could become hostile (that, and the fact they were carrying battering rams, swords, lances, and scythes) and slammed the oak gates in their faces. However, they neglected to shut the West Gate; hence the Abingdon mob merely shuffled a hundred yards to the west and entered Oxford.

The following day, Mayor John de Bereford rode to Woodstock to seek a hunting Edward III and recruit his authority to help stop the rioting. However, de Warenne had left behind an escalating situation as villagers from outside Oxford had communicated a call to arms by ringing local church bells, and several hundred had also entered Oxford and were marching towards the pre-arranged meeting site in St Giles. Once the town reinforcements outnumbered the students, a signal was given to attack the colleges.

The Town side then marched to Beaumont Fields where they slaughtered several students; 'slay', 'havocock' and 'give good knocks' were the reported rallying calls of the townspeople.

After fully two days of rioting, sixty-three students were dead. Horrific accounts detail that some students were scalped by the townspeople. And how many townspeople died? No one knows as, in an illustration of exactly how important the townspeople were considered to be by the University, their death toll was never counted nor recorded.

Just as he'd done following an earlier thirteenth-century riot, the unimpeachably neutral Bishop of Lincoln reported to the King that the riots were entirely the fault of the townspeople (a view that evidently wasn't infringed by being 150 miles away at the time), and he constructively recommended fierce punishments coupled with a reductive approach to the town's already clipped authority, in addition to whatever (hopefully severe) reprisals he was sure the King was already planning to take on the scummy townspeople.

The King, with the predictability of leaves falling in autumn, once again ruled in favour of the Gown, although scholars were suspended from teaching for three years for their part in the student mayhem – which replicated the same punishment handed out after the murderous riots of 1209 when University teaching was also banned via royal and papal decree.

Meanwhile, the Mayor of Oxford had to make annual penitential appearances in the University Church of St Mary's, paying sixty-three pennies (representing each dead student) to the Chancellor, but only until … 1825, when the mayor refused to attend after just 425 years – although the University didn't officially renege their annual claim to the sixty-three pennies until 1955: a mere hardly-bearing-a-grudge-at-all 500 years later.

STAMFORD STAMPEDE

Several Brasenose College students had spent the day customarily studying Aristotle, translating Epictetus and hacking some unfortunate townspeople to death – a day of unswerving normality for most Oxford students in 1334. Only this particular day had eventually deviated from the routine, when a rabble army of townspeople baying for revenge had forcibly stormed through the splintered college gate. Self-preservation, being a great motivator, ensured several students instantly fled Oxford and allowed only time to pack the absolute essentials in their luggage: clothes, money … and a large solid brass doorknocker.

Having reached Stamford in Lincolnshire, the students, led by Philippus de Maniciple, considered this a sufficiently safe distance from the murderous Oxford rabble, and ceremoniously nailed their brass doorknocker on to the entrance of a building requisitioned as their new college. Although the Earl of Warenne offered to sponsor

Brasenose College gate in Stamford, Lincolnshire.

and endow the fledgling university in Stamford, the reigning monarch Edward III did not support the disaffiliated college, and ordered the students to return promptly to Oxford.

In 1890 Brasenose contacted the school in Stamford that inhabited the former site of the breakaway college, enquiring whether they could purchase the doorknocker. Brasenose were informed that the doorknocker was not for sale individually and obtaining it would require purchasing the school. Remarkably, Brasenose purchased the entire school simply to obtain the doorknocker. Which, it should be pointed out, renders Brasenose (literally meaning 'brass-nosed knocker') the only Oxbridge college named after a doorknocker; presumably Brasenose were hoping that having a doorknocker on their entrance would ensure their fellows won several Nobel prizes (see what I did there? No bell … oh, please yourself).

Amazingly, until 1827 it was still mandatory for every Oxford University Master of Arts to swear an oath not to teach in Stamford.

TOWN, GOWN AND CROWN

In 1399 Richard II permitted Oxford University to receive papal exemption from laws, as did Henry IV in 1403 (though not, you notice, the townspeople). Whereas Town and Gown had traditionally battled, the introduction of the monarch's attempt to influence the city's powerbase ensured there was now an unholy trinity of Town, Gown and Crown.

There was already an indecent gulf between the afforded lifestyles of the townspeople and students. And the Crown's role was sometimes manipulated to ensure Gown remained dominant over Town. A salient example occurred when University College were sued in 1361 after they became embroiled in a property dispute and falsely claimed royal exemption, stating that they were Oxford's oldest college and founded by King Alfred.

Several colleges compete for the title of Oxford's oldest – often vociferously, given the oldest Oxford college equates to the oldest college in the English-speaking world. Traditionally the runners and riders are: University College, Balliol, Merton and Teddy Hall, with various self-serving propaganda issued over the centuries – though few have dabbled so darkly in the black arts of PR as University College, who falsified documentation to prove their college was founded by King Alfred.

Forged papers were produced to support this falsehood and were sufficiently well counterfeited to be sanctioned by Richard II. This led to the college having the embarrassing accomplishment of staging their 1,000th anniversary dinner before they celebrated their 750th anniversary dinner in 1999. Not a great vote of confidence for the college's Maths Department.

The college was actually established in 1249 by William of Durham. Although they may not have hosted any students, nor owned a hall of residence until some forty years later, therein lies a gap that allows some rival colleges to squeeze through and claim the title of Oxford's oldest for themselves.

University College.

College founder William had departed the Sorbonne in 1229 following a riot between students and Parisians at a funfair. Arrested at the fair, he served a jail term for throwing a coconut at a dwarf's head – he was just a little shy (oh come on … don't groan).

THREE

THE FIFTEENTH CENTURY

A papal communiqué in 1410 slated Oxford's students, accusing them of 'sleeping all day, rising at night to lurk about taverns and brothels, and are bent on robbing and homicide'. Not an ideal report to take home to your fee-paying parents at the end of term. As a result, the townspeople were banned from housing students as lodgers – which is slightly harsh, blaming the influence of the townspeople for the students' debaucheries. However, the University spin-doctored the papal bull, and stated that if students remained within college walls, then the wicked influences of townspeople could no longer reach and infect them. Nevertheless, the Pope wasn't entirely convinced, so he despatched his own appointed monitor to Oxford, to deliver an investigation into students' 'disgraceful behaviour'.

Actively engaged in just the sort of disgraceful behaviour the Pope had in mind was Merton student Richard Lytham. He was sent down for constantly frequenting brothels, although the King ordered his return to Merton eight years later and insisted that he was made a fellow – which must have made things a bit awkward at high table.

When Archbishop Arundel arrived into Oxford in 1411, holding the capacity of the Pope's inspector to gauge the levels of rumoured debauchery and 'public copulation inherit amongst students and townspeople', he was locked out of St Mary's Church in the High Street. This led to 'several students being soundly whipped to the great satisfaction of Henry IV'.

Given that the century had commenced with the choking grip of the Heresy Act passed in 1401, which rendered the act of a layman reading the Bible by himself unaided by an interpretive clergyman to be an offence punishable by death, this did rather render the times somewhat illiberal – hence Oxford's behaviour was becoming dangerously cavalier.

Indeed, student behaviour was sufficiently cavalier to influence Chaucer's writing, who channelled it into his most famous work. Chaucer may have attended Hart College (now Hertford) in this same period, though definitive proof hovers teasingly beyond reach. The removal of students from lodging houses in the city is referenced in Chaucer's tale of an Oxford scholar who is more interested in studying his landlord's wife in intimate detail than his reading list of prescribed texts.

But there were plentiful students' lodgings available and they continued to be utilised, albeit now illicitly, as by the mid-fifteenth century over seventy academic halls were in existence in Oxford (compared with only thirty-eight surviving colleges today). St Edmund Hall is the sole

Hertford College.

survivor from this period to have evolved into a contemporary college with the original name intact, although its independence went missing for nearly 500 years after falling upon hard times. After retaining only one undergraduate and six fellows, the Provost of neighbouring college Queen's bought Teddy Hall under the pretence that he would enable it to regain its status as a functioning college once the debts had been cleared, yet instead he promptly occupied it as part of Queen's until independence was finally returned in 1957. That explains the intensive rivalry between the two colleges today, and the occasional positioning of 'And now wash your hands' signs on the wall of Queen's that faces Teddy Hall.

Towards the end of the fifteenth century, students were constantly breaking regulations, resulting in college rules being transparently added retrospectively after indiscretions happened that rule-makers lacked the foresight to imagine before occurrence: for example, New College's statutes specifically forbids the playing of ball games in the chapel.

St Edmund Hall.

In 1432 the University published a league table of student offences with matching fines incurred: carrying a weapon = 12d fine, striking person with fist = 4s fine, but with a stone or club (6s), with axe or sword (10s), carrying bow and arrow with intent to harm (20s), gathering an army to inflict bodily injuries (30s). The best value option here is clearly the last one: recruiting a private army to commit multiple murder resulted in a barely-off-putting £1.50 fine if convicted.

NYMPHS OF THE PAVEMENT

Oxford, known for its sizable, unreconstructed bourgeois population – or so is the peddled myth – unsurprisingly found prostitutes too common for its liking. Furthermore, it even found the noun 'prostitute' objectionable, and deployed creative semantics to re-brand them as 'nymphs of the pavement'.

Oxford possessed innumerable areas synonymous with the vice trade, supported by students who were habituate customers; *Rowlandson's Oxford* by A. Hamilton Gibbs reported 'the Dons were in all too many cases the cause of sending recruits to the ranks of the oldest profession in the world. Heads of colleges, reverend clerics, and holders of fellowships must all answer to the charge of wenching'.

The city's principal vice area (which no doubt also included President, Master and Warden vice areas too) was Magpie Lane. Or, to be correct: Grove Lane. Or more correctly: Grope Lane. Or even more correctly: Grope C**t Lane.

The current street name Magpie Lane (connecting Merton Street with the High Street) is a crass re-invention by the timorous authorities. Its previous name was Grove Lane, which was a sanitised version of Grope Lane, but Grope Lane in itself represented a considerable dilution of the street's original title. Think of the most offensive word in the English language beginning with 'C' and then insert it between Grope and Lane, and you have the original name of Magpie Lane. This was not unique to Oxford, as London, and many provincial towns, would possess a similarly named street representative of the town's red-light area, thereby causing A-Z compilers to blush redder than the lights on display in those streets.

This was only one of several examples of future councils changing streets to more sanitised names. St Helen's Passageway was originally christened Hell's Passage, the implication being that it lead to hell aka the Turf Tavern – once a self-styled den of inequity, renowned for student gaming, carding, cock-fighting and boozy debauchery. These activities, particularly the cock-fighting, were licensed by the Chancellor of the University, who received rents and commission.

Whereas some colleges received funding from such dubious activities in the fifteenth century (naming no names), other colleges were extremely puritanical.

St John the Baptist Hospital, operational until the mid-fifteenth century, and whose ruins sit underneath the foundations of Magdalen College Tower and the college's appropriately named St John the Baptist Quad, issued a decree that 'lascivious and pregnant women are forbidden from entering this hospital' – which must have meant their maternity ward failed to hit its annual patient targets.

CHANCELLOR OF THE SEX CHECKER

In an attempt to ensure Oxford remained a stiflingly moral environment, the University's Chancellor wielded substantial power on the town, able to close down shops, revoke trade licenses and approve weights and measures, seemingly without anything more legally justifiable than a whim. He also possessed authority to imprison townswomen in a specially designed prostitutes' pen named The Maiden's Chamber, often convicted on little more evidence for prostitution than simply being on a pavement after 9 p.m.

He even obtained authority to set the price of bread in Oxford's shops and markets, a power that lasted almost until the end of the

Lincoln College.

free ivy beer. This is not poisoned ivy, offered as a retaliatory gesture to kill a few more students – but ground ivy. Its presence is intended to alter the taste and result in less being consumed, but these are students who'd willingly be drinking mouthwash for its alcoholic properties if there wasn't free ivy beer available that lunchtime.

Not that free beer necessarily placates the bubbling rivalry between Lincoln and Brasenose. Recently a Lincoln student put Brasenose College up for sale on eBay, listing the item as 'an Oxford College surplus to requirements: going cheap', adding the further description 'a used item since 1509 so generally in quite worn condition'. Bidding reached over £1m before the item was forcibly removed from the auction site, and the college authorities fined the prankster £50. His additional punishment was to read the Latin grace in Brasenose before formal hall one evening – phew, that'll teach him!

FIRE WARDEN

Oxford students have always retained an inexplicable attraction towards bonfires. Merton's head of college, the Warden, locked out his college's entire student population on 5 November 1865 and wouldn't let them back inside for two days, after students had lit an enormous bonfire in the quad.

Although illicit bonfires in college quadrangles continued to be a frequently encountered problem throughout the nineteenth and early twentieth century, at least these were undeniably trivial offences when compared to earlier fifteenth-century Oxford practices. In 1423 the head of St Edmund Hall, Principal William Taylor, was added to the bonfire and burnt alive for being a Lollard; no, not an effigy, but the actual Principal himself! In person and alive (well, initially). *ovch*

PRIME CRIME SHRINE FINE

In 1469 a student from Beam Hall in Merton Street was caught chiselling expensive jewels from St Frideswide's shrine; his punishment, for the double crime of jewel heist and desecrating the tomb of Oxford's patron saint was … being merely informed that he would now have to take a slightly lower degree! Not that the University's authority figures demonstrated impeccable role-model attributes: in 1452 Robert Wrixham of St George's Hall, along with a hired accomplice, broke into the house of an Oxford fishmonger and proceeded to rob and violently assault him with large wooden clubs and a bronze church candlestick; Robert Wrixham was the college chapel's priest.

FOUR

THE SIXTEENTH CENTURY

In the sixteenth century Trinity College students ordered a call to arms to storm the citadel of St John's after a Trinity student had been ambushed in an apparently motiveless attack whilst walking through an orchard populated by St John's students. He was stoned with unripe apples, prior to being left naked and prostrate with a half inserted apple lodged in his mouth like an over-ready hog. The unfortunate student then endured the further undignified act of having an apple shoved up his other end. A mass brawl subsequently broke out in St John's front quad following a Trinity invasion.

Trinity vs. St Johns

St John's College.

Those who fear that today's youth are currently the high-water mark of unacceptable behaviour should be aware that this incident occurred in the late sixteenth century. And St John's weren't even Trinity's main rival – that unenviable post was always willingly assumed by Balliol.

NAVIGATING THE OXFORD CARNAL

Student Robert Smith of Magdalen College had become known to the University authorities by 1582, and was denied his degree for 'gathering lewd company in college and guilt of the most shameful crimes as carnal copulation'. Which means (once the puritanically freighted rhetoric has been decontaminated) that he was probably up before the authorities for having sex with his girlfriend. Smith, understandably, considered this a harsh course of events and immediately instigated an appeal – which resulted in him discovering that he had no right of appeal!

JAILHOUSE SHOCK

The practice of attending lectures inside colleges with assigned tutors to individual students didn't become a commonly adopted innovation until the Elizabethan age. Soon afterwards, a pattern began to emerge where Oxford educated those going into the clergy, whilst others rode the newly embraced acceptability of prescribed teaching leading towards more secular career choices, obtaining a grounding in natural history, classics, rhetoric, logic and rioting – as Town and Gown battles continued. Corpus Christi considered Oxford sufficiently hazardous to rule that students were only permitted to walk in groups of three or more. Yet there was one enemy faced by Town and Gown that was to prove even more fearsome and deadly than each other: plague.

The plague broke out in 1563. Oxford's term was suspended in 1564, 1571 and 1572. In 1574 typhus spread from an outbreak in Oxford Jail via prisoners to judge and jury, then to townspeople and students.

Plague ensured that the University could expand their imperial empire throughout the town by colonising town properties after the plague had killed the inhabitants. University men were able to return to their country retreats – the word 'rustication', that still enjoys a modern usage as the term deployed for any student temporarily suspended for bad behaviour, literally means 'to return to the countryside'. Since departure to one's other place in the country wasn't an option for most peasants, surfs and labourers, their unavoidable destiny was to stay in Oxford and catch the plague. This explains how Jesus College, so central that it practically is the centre of Oxford, managed to arrive in 1571 and occupy such a vast swathe of central real estate: the locals had all been eradicated by the plague.

So the townspeople invented a revengeful game traditionally played against Jesus College at Christmas. A longstanding act of Town revenge on Gown is to ring up the porter of Jesus on 25 December. As soon as he answered, callers simply enquired 'is that Jesus?' When the porter replied in the affirmative, the caller wished him a 'Happy Birthday'!

Fellows' Library, Jesus College.

STUDENT CAUGHT GETTING HIS ORGAN OUT

Magdalen students, including John Foxe, stripped the college chapel of candlesticks, paintings, altar pieces and anything else that was remotely removable. Boston-born (that's East Coast as in Lincolnshire, not Massachusetts) Foxe, who went on to travel around the country witnessing people being burnt alive and wrote a best-selling book about it (*The Book of Martyrs*), even succeeded in crow-barring the chapel organ off the wall and removing it into the quad, where the students smashed it. Faced with severe recriminations from the college authorities, Foxe and his fellow vandals claimed that they were acting out of religious duty, and were merely exercising their Protestant loathing of decorative High Church leanings. It would be harder to get away with that excuse nowadays after a spot of drunken student vandalism.

Magdalen College.

MERTON MAN

Merton College's official visitor forced an imposed appointment upon the college in 1562 when John Man arrived as the new Warden. However, the Merton students steadfastly refused to let him into the college for several days, resulting in a quaint tradition still continued today whereby any newly appointed Warden has to witness the main college gates being slammed in their face, prior to knocking again to seek admission.

MY NAME IS EARL

The Earl of Leicester's appointment as Chancellor of the University was not generally popular amongst students, especially after the earl had used his opening address to promulgate that he would no longer tolerate 'Oxford's streets fuller of scholars than townsmen' nor 'the ale houses full all day and much of the night with scholars tippling, dicing, carding and worse occupied'. Spoilsport. It's the 'worse' which is particularly intriguing.

His fulmination continued: 'rather than partaking of good learning and education in Oxford, they lerned nothing but how to tipple in taverns, returning to their friends after Oxford less lerned than when they came and worse mannered than if they had been long conversant with the worse sort of people instead'. Crickey! Even so, most students would have left Oxford having learnt that 'learnt' is the correct past tense of the verb 'to learn' – something the hubristic Chancellor clearly hadn't 'lerned'. I blame the drink – and worse.

THE BRIDGE OF SCYTHES

Finding a student who prefers drinking milk to alcohol is about as easy as spotting the mock April Fool story in the 1 April edition of the

Sunday Sport. Yet Mr Jones, a student residing in Turl Street, favoured such a drink. When he suspected that his milk was being watered down by the provider, he visited the culpable shop at night and removed the door, painstakingly unscrewing the hinges by candlelight with a paid accomplice to find out (wouldn't it have been easier to write a letter?).

Later, he met his future wife during a Town and Gown riot, which must have been a distracting environment to nurture romance!

Not all student participation in rioting delivered such a happy ending. Brasenose student Mervyn Prower holds the unenviable distinction of being the very last Oxford student to be killed in a Town and Gown riot, murdered with a butcher's hook in 1851.

Another student was killed in Holywell Street, hanged for being a highwayman (well, he had to supplement his student grant somehow), and the area subsequently became known among the townspeople as the Gown's Gallows.

This was not such an unusual choice of profession, as Brasenose student John Clavell adopted the same line of part-time work. After coming up to Oxford in 1619, Clavell immediately stole the college's plate. Caught and subsequently pardoned, Clavell remained stubbornly unreceptive to any crime-doesn't-pay-lessons, as he then became a highwayman. Caught and subsequently pardoned again (this time by the King), he was able to step out of death row due to regal clemency, and subsequently wrote appalling plays and novels that must have implored critics to dismiss the King's misguided leniency.

FIVE

THE SEVENTEENTH CENTURY

In the early seventeenth century, Oxford witnessed a theological division between Calvinists and soteriologist Arminians. Each group fought to donate more books representative of each partisan doctrine to libraries and enrol more students sympathetic to their views. At least the rules of engagement had now switched to intellectual rather than physical – although that would inevitably change. Initially dismissive of each other in debate, this spread to acute division. Clearly, Oxford thought, a suppressive creed was required that would be consistently mad and unfair for everyone – and in William Laud, they knew someone who could provide it.

LAUD ABOVE

William Laud wrote the Laudian Code, a dogmatic diatribe composed in Latin, which was considered so sagacious it lasted for fully 200 years after its publication in 1636, serving as the unchallenged rules for Oxford University's governance of students and, given that they controlled them too, the townspeople.

One paragraph decrees:

Scholars and graduates of all conditions are to keep away during the day, and especially at night, from the shops and houses of the townsmen; but particularly from houses where women of ill or suspected fame or harlots are kept or harboured, whose company is peremptorily forbidden to all scholars whatever, either in their private rooms or in the houses of citizens.

Noticeably, this is hardly airtight when it comes to inventive law students looking for interpretative legal loopholes to visit the occasional harlot; forbidden physical entanglement 'in private rooms or house of citizens' surely renders the student perpetrators untouchable if student and harlot are entwined in monkey loving against the bottle bank behind Wetherspoons or in, say, a brothel – the latter appearing to be an exempt category.

The Laudian Code enforced a huge list of rules, informing students not to have long hair, not to wear clothes that aren't dark, not to hunt with ferrets, not to deviate from his highly specific interpretation of ecumenical matters, not to frequent a shop that sells tobacco or herbs, even if such goods are not the main trade of the shop. If students break any of these rules, then 'he shall be flogged in public'. Very reasonable: so a student discovered in a shop that sells marjoram and wine (i.e. Sainsbury's) will be publicly whipped. Meanwhile, any townspeople caught fencing (err … that's the sport with thin swords and a bee-keeper's mask, not receiving stolen goods) or committing the monstrous act of dancing or using a rope 'are to be incarcerated'.

Other parts of the code are just gloriously prejudicial: 'abstain from that absurd practice of walking publicly in boots'. Remarkably this rule was enforced and Lincoln College's records show that their Rector fined student George Ashton 12*d* for wearing boots. Ashton was outraged by the fine, refused to pay, and was promptly given three days' notice prior to being booted out (yep, intended that one) of college.

Laud lords it over everyone, reserving particular splenetic dislike towards professional showmen, actors, singers and falconers. Clearly all students must be banned from seeing anything in case it caused them to sin, or even contemplate sin.

Eventually seemingly everything else was banned by Archbishop William Laud, who continued to write indefatigable legislation randomly outlawing students participating in just about anything: playing chess, keeping a rabbit, owning a comb, liking ribbon, sneezing on a Tuesday, using words containing vowels (OK, may have got a bit Laudian myself with a couple there). Although it should be noted, bear baiting and cock fighting were NOT banned, but considered perfectly acceptable bordering upon mandatory.

By the end Laud risked making Hitler look like a liberal, care-free hippy: 'students shall not walk about the City of Oxford, or its suburbs, or the streets, or the markets, or Carfax,' which is slightly limiting.

He even banned any colourful clothes and a further decree was issued that wigs were also banned, as were re-enactments of gladiators(!)

Laud ordered magistrates to suppress the taverns, and by 1626 only five public houses remained open in the whole of Oxford.

Anyone with hair long enough to reach their ears was forcibly ejected from Oxford, including senior fellows from Magdalen, Balliol and Oriel, in addition to numerous student dismissals. Other perceived misdemeanours resulted in equally brazenly dispensed justice – with one scholar expelled from Oxford for 'knowingly placing a cross inside Lincoln College chapel'; you'd have to say that was harsh.

An additional rule was then passed that students were 'not permitted to lounge or linger in shops of tradesmen, mechanics or in markets'. So much for encouraging the browsing culture.

Laud removed and subsequently banished from Oxford three students (one from Magdalen and two attending Balliol) for 'seditious preaching and liking spurs' (Laud was clearly a massive Arsenal fan). As if this gesture wasn't sufficiently intolerant, Laud then dismissed several proctors for allowing this to happen – a spurious logic, similar to disbanding the police whenever a crime is committed.

He had successfully concentrated power to the University, but by 1641 Laud's years of tirelessly making enemies had caught up with him, and he was impeached for high treason. Evidence against him was presented by Nathaniel Brent, the Warden of Merton, and Laud was eventually executed in 1645.

Hopefully whoever arranged his funeral ensured all attendant mourners were attired in compulsory colourful esoteric fashions, long-haired wigs and spurred boots, with actors and rope-dancers booked as the pallbearers. A falconry and gladiators' display after the graveside benediction would have been a nice touch too.

Amazingly, the Laudian Code somehow survived as the cornerstone of the University's laws until 1854.

GETTING ON YOUR WICK

Fires, either started deliberately due to religious intolerance or accidentally to provide candlelight for nocturnal study, were a common student danger for several centuries. However, Christ Church student Thomas Hill reduced the chances of his college being burnt down by a carelessly neglected naked candle. In 1657 a student from rival college Pembroke bet him a guinea that he could not eat a pound of wax candles in one evening. He did, and he could almost certainly have burnt his candle from both ends throughout most of the next day. Challenge

DUEL INTENTION

Thomas Coryate attended Worcester College, became court jester to James I's son Prince Henry, and undertook a tour of Europe, which innovated the practice later to become known as the Grand Tour. Coryate walked a huge proportion of 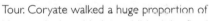his round-trip to Venice, published the flamboyantly portentous book *Coryat's Crudities: Hastily gobbled up in Five Month's Travels in France and Italy* that John Donne mocked for its pomposity (that's akin to Van Gogh mocking your lack of ears), and is remembered as the man who first introduced the table fork and umbrella to Britain.

He packed a lot into his relatively short life (he died of dysentery in India in 1617 aged thirty nine), including surviving a duel with another student who accused him of harbouring lustful feelings towards his sister. Coryate simply did not turn up for the duel, as he'd sensibly brought the departure date forward and had already embarked on his travels.

COURTING STUDENTS

University proctors policed the town's taverns after a decree was passed in the late seventeenth century by the Chancellor's Court permitting publicans to be fined if they were discovered serving undergraduates. Evident difficulty in recognising everyone who was an undergraduate, coupled with the direct contradiction of a business owner's profit instinct, rendered this law unenforceable, although several gavels were duly banged in the University court before the rule was revoked.

WHO WEARS THE TROUSERS IN THIS RELATIONSHIP

A woman dressed as a man entered Hart College (now Hertford) as an undergraduate in 1617, but her disguise was almost instantly discovered. However, a female succeeded with the same rouse at St Edmund Hall, where her true gender remained undiscovered for over a year until she became pregnant with a child fathered by her roommate: a gentleman commoner. Upon discovery of the pregnancy, both were sent down immediately, and 'the poor ruined girl was taken in by a kindly townswoman in Cornmarket'.

Ironically, nearly three full centuries later, as Oxford reluctantly approached the enlightened twentieth century, a St Hugh's female undergraduate was sent down 'for dressing like a man' (i.e. charged and found guilty of the hideous crime of regularly wearing trousers!)

OLIVER'S ARMY

Following Cromwell's Civil War victory, the puritans planned to close down Oxford and Cambridge, preferring to start another university elsewhere; that decision subsequently led to the origins of England's only other collegiate university: Durham.

Having installed himself as Chancellor, Cromwell then ordered students to inform on any deviation from the newly seared official view overheard in daily prayers or sermons. Students were briefed that they would receive rewards for informing on other students, though it was unclear what those rewards were, given that the Puritans had energetically banned seemingly everything.

Yet the Interregnum was willingly supported by many scholars. Students attending Teddy Hall in 1678 fired muskets at an effigy of the Pope, prior to filling the pontiff with fireworks, and then threw him on a noisy quadrangle bonfire. When the college authorities saw this spectacle, they immediately sprang into action, approached the perpetrators … and offered them a perfectly reasonable claret.

Not that Cromwell's move towards abstention and Puritanism wasn't considered unjust in some areas of Oxford life. Another St Edmund Hall student complained 'banning gaming, drinking, hunting and wenching makes Oxford life intolerable', However, students continued to regularly attend cock fighting in Holywell Street and bull baiting in St Clements; that's an historical truth – not just a cock and bull story.

A dispute soon broke out between the High Church head of Queen's College and students with more Cromwellian leanings. The Provost merely upped the tension by fining students and fellows for various randomly invented indiscretions, including 'insufficient sermon delivery time in college chapel'. One Queen's underling, John Langhorne, refused to comply and threatened 'to stiletto' the Provost of Queen's in what must qualify as one of the most gloriously camp threats every issued.

But the townspeople were still suffering, even with the Puritans now ruling the University. Earlier, in 1612, townspeople recorded their grievances to an unsympathetic University that proctors, aided by the occasional student accomplice, had regularly broken into their homes and imprisoned people or possessions until payment of 'whatever sums of money the proctors do so desire'. Nice little extortion and kidnapping racket the University had going there.

BOD A JOB

Elizabethan diplomat Thomas Bodley created the Bodlein Library in 1602, and resuscitated the previous library that had occupied the site from decades of decline and a likely death. Francis Bacon (no, not the painter – the other one) was moved to describe the resulting library as 'an ark to save learning from the deluge'. Both the scale and success of the library were huge: it houses to this day 10,000 medieval manuscripts. Its importance ensured rigid safekeeping and every student and staff member using the library has had to affirm an oath ever since: 'I hereby undertake not to bring into the Library, or kindle therein, any fire or flame.' Disappointingly, students are now permitted to affirm the oath via e-mail!

Not that the Bod was always this vigilant against fire; in 1683 they conducted a policy of positively encouraging pyromania. A decree was issued by the University that a public burning would be staged in Old Schools Quad where the assembled works of poet and assiduous pamphleteer John Milton would be burnt by students (they wanted to burn Milton himself, but he was presumably unavailable).

DEMANDING PROOF

Anthony Ashley Cooper, Lord Chancellor to Charles II and founder of the Whig Party, was a student at Exeter College, coming up in 1637. The head of college attempted to weaken the beer available in the college bar as it was a destructively strong proof. Cooper, whose name implied a professional interest in beer barrels and their contents, was outraged by such suggested irresponsibility and organised a student strike until the potently proofed ale was restored to the students' bar.

This serves as an illustrative insight into Oxford University's value system. In the 1680s Trinity received a fortuitous windfall when a former fellow bequeathed them a substantial endowment. Meeting to

Exeter College.

discuss how the money should be invested, they rejected adding more scholarships, teaching posts, lectures rooms, library books, and instead blew the entire endowment on expanding the college's already swollen wine cellar – to such an extent that it collapsed the foundations of the main hall, necessitating a rebuild!

However, most colleges, and Exeter in particular after Anthony Cooper's victory, did struggle with the problem of drunken students. One plan, initiated in the late nineteenth-century age of temperance, saw Exeter College launch an Essay Writing Club, which they hoped would provide a preferable and more intellectually nutritious alternative to drinking; unsurprisingly, the club failed to survive into the twentieth century.

WOOD WORK

Anthony Wood was a prolific diarist, and a generous dollop of historians' current knowledge of seventeenth-century Oxford is dependent on Wood's abundant observations. Not that his naturally controversial style enabled him to live an enemy-free existence – although Wood's astringency in his later work can in part be explained by encroaching deafness. In 1678 his house was searched by the authorities for any written materials that 'may be deemed treasonous'. Later, after Wood had promulgated that a Chancellor had accepted bribes from venal students in return for University positions and degrees, Wood's works were publicly burnt outside the Sheldonian Theatre. Students, whose pyromaniac tendencies were unchained whenever there was such an opportunity for a good public burning (Bumps suppers, Guy Fawkes, illicit quad bonfires), willingly participated, ensuring the fire nearly went out of control and risked torching Christopher Wren's early masterpiece.

UNCIVIL WAR

Over 300 students responded to a call to arms by the Royalist army and attended a drilling session for volunteers held in Christ Church's Tom Quad in 1642. Diarist Anthony Wood was present and recounted that the students all left sharply as soon as it started to rain, oblivious to the shouted instructions of their drill sergeant. Yet several students joined the Royalist army later and remained defending Oxford.

After Charles I had been living in Christ Church for two years, a siege by the surrounding Parliamentarians was making life increasingly desperate for both the University and King, and on 27 April 1646 Charles I, accompanied by his Groom of the Royal Bedchamber, slipped through Canterbury Gate and departed Christ Church, having disguised himself to look like a servant by shaving off his flowing curly locks. Of course, three years later he was to have more than his hair cut off.

NO SMOKING IN BED

Most students in the seventeenth century were tooled up whenever appearing in public. A 1619 record confirms that student John Newdigate kept a full length sword, musket ball shot, crossbows, arrows, pike and a large pile of gunpowder under his bed.

TALL TAILS

In 1674 Mark Coleman of Christ Church reported a fellow student to the proctors for 'eating my horse' (ever started to eat a whole horse only to discover that you weren't as hungry as you thought?). When asked by the University authorities if he'd

witnessed the accused eating his horse, he replied that he had 'and even saw the tail hanging out of the student's mouth'.

SCARY CROW

Pubs, topped only by rioting, provided the most popular activities that enabled Town and Gown to interact, and students weren't always particularly fussy in their choice of local. One notoriously rough public house, The Split Crow, was situated outside Balliol; unsurprisingly, this attracted such numerous Balliol students that the Master was forced to issue the proclamation: 'a pub only frequented by draymen and tinkers who have let their reputation go, and hence not suitable for Balliol men'. The Master's proclamation apparently caused a surge in Balliol students visiting the pub, now attracted by its newly illicit status.

SIX

THE EIGHTEENTH CENTURY

By the start of the eighteenth century, Oxford's academic reputation was in indisputable decline, with a narrow and frequently familiar set of examination questions required for obtaining an Oxford degree. Not only was the range of questions extremely limited, they were also easily obtainable, routinely bought and sold throughout the city's coffee houses. Due to their reputation for hosting enlightened conversation, Oxford's coffee houses were known as 'the penny universities', albeit simultaneously masquerading as the guinea degrees whenever anyone wanted to buy their Finals paper.

Nor were the University's building priorities necessarily academic in outlook either: there was vast support amongst fellows and students for the Clarendon Building to be erected, not as a flagship University book press, but as a purpose-built riding school, which offered a telling insight into the University's value system given several students and dons lobbied to teach not science and the arts, but dressage skills.

However, the eighteenth century did see a thawing of the University's formal discipline (the long-standing rule forbidding students to converse whilst dining in any language other than Latin was now no longer practiced. But the students ensured there was still plentiful indiscipline.

FOOTE SOLDIER

Samuel Foote came up to Worcester College in 1737 and immediately became well acquainted with the University proctors for serial

Worcester College.

misdemeanours, and was regularly accustomed to being gated. One evening, returning from a May Day ball that he had not been invited to, he was spotted by the proctors as his stagecoach flashed past them speeding along the High Street being pulled by a team of six; whilst his right hand fought with the reigns, his left hand was hungrily groping a struggling prostitute. For this offence the University authorities ensured Foote was permanently sent down from Oxford: he was charged with appearing in public without wearing his regulation gown and cap!

GIVE US A CAUDLE

Public oratory was both a required and acquired skill during an undergraduate's Oxford tenure. Throughout the eighteenth century, students would be expected to read aloud during dinner from the Bible or Homer (Mmmm ... dinner). Colleges established a Candlemas Day tradition where on each 2 February every freshman was expected to deliver a speech in the main hall to an audience comprised of the college's collective undergraduates, fellows and staff, whilst both speaker and audience alike hung around wishing John Logie Baird would hurry up and get a move on.

Not that television can justifiably claim to be a perfect replacement for oratory: as proof, let's call the first witness for the prosecution: reality television. 'Reality television' is a bizarre oxymoronic name, given that there is probably nothing more conceptionally opposite to reality that the environ, behaviour and set up of shows such as *Big Brother* and *I'm A Celebrity Get Me Out of Here*.

Ironically Oxford University students can justifiably claim to have influenced, if not outrightly invented, the humiliating proto-type of *I'm A Celebrity Get Me Out of Here*. A Shrove Tuesday event that was already a standard annual occurrence by the mid-eighteenth century, having probably originated at Merton College a century before, saw undergraduates obligated to present mandatory speeches in front of the assembled college personnel. Earlier a chef, with borderline psychotic tendencies, had brewed a horrendous caudle (a type of gruel) filled with rancid mouldy fish oil, the sort of anti-gastro concoction that would result in an on-air Gordon Ramsey tasting prompting so many bleeps that listeners would mistake the broadcast for a Morse code message. Glasses of water and beer were also provided with the caudle. Should a speaker be voted a hit, then he could partake of a regular drink. If his contemporaries voted the performance uninspiring and dull, then caudle was consumed. Did I mention that the rotten caudle was also laced with vomit-inducing quantities of salt?

The renowned diarist Anthony Wood records in his published journals a speech he delivered at the 1648 event. Opening with 'May it please your Gravities to admit into your presence a kitten of muses, and a mere frog of Lexicon to croak the cataracts of his slumberous cererosity before your sagacious ingenuities.'You may wish to speculate on whether he received a stinky salty drink.

WELSH DRAGOON

A play staged at the King's Arms pub included a scene requiring a burly actor playing a Cornishman to wrestle with three Welshman in succession, winning each bout. After felling the scripted third and expected final Welshman, the actor delivered his line 'have you any more Welshmen?', prompting a Welsh student from Jesus College to mount the stage and require the mock Cornishman to conduct another – now real, as opposed to pretend – fight; the actor was overcome by the unscripted fourth wrestling Welshman, thus proving why the play had imposed a sensible three Welshmen wresting limit.

OXFORD CHAIR OF WOMEN'S STUDIES

The Laudian Code was still tightly applied by some fun-disapproving University authorities, even as late as the 1770s. Hence in 1775, when a small group of undergraduates wanted to indulge in a party with (shock, horror) women present, they realised that it could never be hosted in Oxford. Unfortunately, it could not be hosted elsewhere either – particularly in the small Oxfordshire village of Eaton.

Unbeknown to the party hopefuls, the University officials had been monitoring the undergraduates' planning from an early stage. On the intended night of the party in Eaton, just as the hired dancing girls had entered the room to begin their performance, the assembled students saw a series of torch beams shining through the curtains. The sudden, port-spluttering realisation that the party house was completely surrounded by University marshals, bull dogs and proctors meant that the students engaged in the apparently impossible task of identifying hiding places in a small house. Within a few minutes, the students were rounded up and the semi-naked dancing girls wrapped in blankets – with the exception of one student who somehow avoided detection.

A few days later, the lone escapee received a note in his pigeon hall requesting him to see the head of college at once. Fearing a possible rustication for his illicit indulgence, he knocked on the door harbouring some trepidation, but was relieved to discover that he was not about to be punished, as 'the mode of escape was so ingenious that I am reluctant to punish you and therefore wish you good morning'. The clever concealment had been provided by a dancing girl, who draped him with a curtain to form a makeshift settee that they sat on whilst being interviewed by the party-busting proctors.

APPROPRIATELY NAMED VICE CHANCELLOR

In 1778 the appropriately named Vice Chancellor (given his penchant for regulating vice) caught several proctors drunk in Oxford's pubs – the same pubs that the proctors were charged with monitoring to ensure that no University personnel were frequenting them.

Students visiting Oxford's pubs would inevitably lead to confrontations with the townspeople anxious to draw territorial disputes. What appeared to be a more erudite meeting occurred in The Mite in 1782, when several amassed theology students encountered some townspeople who were keen to debate ecumenical matters. However, after two hours spent discussing transubstantiation, a local vicar requested that a waiter bring him a Bible in order to illustrate his point. When the waiting staff arrived with a large church Bible, the clergyman used it to club a student over the head! Predictably, this led to a students v. townspeople bar brawl. The most violent protagonist was then later arrested, a few yards further down the High Street from the by now somewhat wrecked Mitre – after he had conducted the morning service in St Mary's Church!

SCHOOLGIRL ERROR

Not all students were necessarily equipped for a fight. Worcester College student Mr Gower returned to college in a trembling state of agitation one evening in 1756, and reported how he had been ruthlessly mugged and assaulted by a violent band of cut-throat townspeople in the lane known today as St Helen's Passage. Following investigations by the proctors, the mugger turned out to be a ten-year-old girl working without an accomplice. She was sentenced to six weeks hard labour, while Mr Gower was probably sentenced to receive considerably more than six weeks of dining hall ridicule.

GOSPEL STORY

In 1761 several students bet Oriel College scholar William Dyer that he couldn't down three pints of wine and then legibly copy out a passage from the New Testament. Carefully ensuring his seat was comfortable, he sat down at a tavern table and purposefully laid out his pen, ink, paper and New Testament. Complying with the bet, he opened the Gospel of Matthew, drank three pints of wine within ten minutes and then, once he had regained consciousness several hours later, was informed by his challengers that he owed them half a crown.

Oriel College.

SERVITUDE

Trinity student Henry Knolys was sent down from Oxford for the crime of 'laughing once in college' in 1707. Harsh.

A far more deserved expulsion happened to aristocrat Walter Savage Lendor – Savage being both his genuine middle name and a rather fitting tmesis. A Trinity student was holding a party, which, according to witnesses, was observed 'as being a quiet and reserved affair' with mainly timid intellectuals present, when Lendor saw an opportunity to try out his new rifle. He complained that the host of the party in a room directly across the quad was a 'particularly scholarly sort' (i.e. 'nerd' in today's parlance). Seeing the party's host open a window, he next observed him ducking for cover as a shower of Lendor's bullets exploded into the walls and shattered a punch bowl. On being permanently dismissed from college, an unapologetic Lendor complained that his intended victims were 'merely servitudes and riff raff' and therefore wouldn't have counted as murder victims. Nice guy.

Being a 'servitude' remained for several centuries the only possible entry route into Oxford for those without a scholarship or cash – a

Trinity
College.

student could attend Oxford for virtually no fee if he was prepared to work as a college servant between his studies. The position and name had originated in Wadham the century before. When the designation ended in the nineteenth century, so did the ability of the poor to attend Oxford – and evidently their ability to be considered legitimate hunting targets by the upper classes.

The direct opposite of servitude would have been a 'first order' or 'nobleman' – these students were usually the sons of barons, knights or earls and, in return for higher fees, they received considerable student privileges and pampering, such as permission to dine at high table. They received better wine, food, prettier prostitutes and larger rooms; this group were more prone to drunkenness, gout, syphilis and agoraphobia accordingly.

Bizarrely, a nobleman would sometimes be indirectly responsible for a poor person gaining a place at Oxford, since a father sending a son to University would sometimes pluck an estate worker to accompany them. Fathers saw this as investing in a spy to observe their son's conduct. One such father advised his son on going up to St John's in the 1780s: 'avoid the company of drinkers, tobacco takers, talkers and swearers.'

Several noblemen complained that they had merely been sent to Oxford or Cambridge in order to seek beneficial relationships for later life. This practice would eventually die out in … OK, so it probably hasn't yet … think BBC, think the City, think the Cabinet, think Oxford Review and Cambridge Footlights.

TAKING CREDIT

A departing student authored a monograph in 1795 titled, rather pompously, *A Few General Directions for the Conduct of a Young Gentleman at Oxford*. In it he states that 'money is useless in Oxford'. This refers to the town tradesmen aligning in a pact to sell exclusively on credit, for which an extortionate interest rate was charged. It was known as the 'townspeople's revenge' against students.

But students weren't just in danger from the townspeople – sometimes their own head of college represented a sinister threat. In 1739 Wadham's warden fled Britain following a charge of rape filed by a male undergraduate. He may have possessed a Woodhousian name in Mr Thistlethwayte, but there was nothing charming about the man since strong accumulated evidence signposted his guilt. Another fellow also implicated in the scandal left Britain, though the college steadfastly refused to comply with the authorities' attempted investigation, further damaging the University's public perception. Numerous pamphleteering resulted.

DOCTOR'S ORDERS

Pembroke College's records confirm that Samuel Johnston single-handedly sunk three bottles of port while dining at the college one evening – and no, they're unlikely to have been miniatures.

PRESIDENTIAL REDRESS

When Corpus Christi student Dr Randolph was discovered by the President to have been regularly truant from college chapel services, a permanent expulsion from Oxford appeared unavoidable. It was compulsory for all members of college to attend chapel, and that included serving staff too. When Randolph was approached by the college head, who opened the conversation by barking, 'no one remains in my college if they don't attend chapel,' it looked like his dismissal was imminent.

Randolph tried a desperate poker bluff, and responded with, 'well, I didn't see you in chapel on Thursday, Sir'.

'What? How dare you – I always attend … oh, that's right. Sorry, I was unavoidably absent on Thursday. I say, old chap, would you like a spot of tea and Madeira cake in my lodgings?' Randolph's luck was most definitely in, as Thursday evening song had been the first time in over three years that the President had missed a chapel service.

FREE PAYING COLLEGE

Edward Drax Free came up to St John's College in the 1780s, and surprised several fellows by surviving a disciplinary hearing with his college place intact after he had lunged violently at the bursar.

Throughout this period of the college's history, a rule had been installed providing a St John's fellow with the tenure of a parish church should that parish be owned by the college. Given St John's expansive land portfolio, several churches fell into this remit, and Free claimed the parish of Sutton, Bedfordshire. Unfortunately, he also claimed the housemaid that went with the vicarage, and immediately impregnated her.

Lacking a similar enthusiasm for preaching, he rarely gave services. Any overtly optimistic parishioners with a lingering hope that services may return to the village were provided with an unambiguous visual clue that this was unlikely when Free stripped the lead off the church roof, sold the bell for scrap and converted the graveyard into a livestock farm.

Intent on claiming everyone in the village as his enemy, he even cheated on his pregnant housemaid by conspiring to impregnate two other local servants who had unwisely consented to more than casual employment at the vicarage.

Attempts to oust him were slow in getting started, and it wasn't a case of the villagers not being able to see the wood for the trees (Free felled all 300 magnificent oaks in the churchyard to sell them as timber), but because Free would drink heavily and then stand at the top of the church tower with a loaded musket.

In 1817 Free unearthed an archaic law left from Elizabeth I's reign and discovered that Catholics could be fined for not attending church services. Hence Free posted invoices itemising £20 per month for

Canterbury
Quad,
St John's
College.

every church service missed. Local landowner Montague Burgoyne, aware that Free was merely raising money to spend on alcohol and prostitutes, refused to pay, citing the somewhat justifiable claim that there were no church services. Montague also campaigned that Free was unfit for the clergy, which eventually saw Free removed from the post after he had been found guilty of lewd conduct, drunkenness and debauchery.

Defrocked and stripped of his church and vicarage, Free decided to encamp himself in the roofless building. Whenever his many creditors arrived, or senior clergymen anxious to reclaim their parish church, he would fire his musket at them from the bell tower. A plan was thus hatched to surround the church and seal down siege conditions. After two weeks, Free was forced to abandon his church (he could probably have survived fourteen days without food, yet the lack of booze and prostitutes for two weeks was tellingly decisive).

Unsurprisingly, St John's declined his request to return as a fellow, and Free died in 1843 in suspicious circumstances after the wheels had been loosened on a stagecoach – surely the eighteenth-century equivalent of cutting someone's brake cable.

SEVEN

THE NINETEENTH CENTURY

By the beginning of the nineteenth century, Oxford had begun aspiring towards a propagation of learning and the University's academia flowered, though not quite everyone had become swept up in this new momentum.

Thomas Dibdin, an early nineteenth-century student at St John's College, complained about the 'fashionable emphasis on studying and examinations' in a letter home to his parents. Not such an emphasis for the rapacious Dibdin though, who was fined and eventually rusticated for breaking windows of rival colleges. His excuse, that he was trying to break into rooms to find women for sex when drunk, undoubtedly increased the severity of his punishment as well as comfortably making the 'Top ten worse student excuses in Oxford's history' list.

Dragging the University into the modern age inevitably meant that there were conservative academics defiantly clinging to Oxford's decorative gothic past, but the modernist momentum eventually pulled them forward.

St Catherine's geographical isolation quietly ensured it didn't attract a dangerous college rivalry, whereas Keble had the misfortunate to border the sixteenth-century opulence of St John's – Keble required land from its neighbour before it could be founded in 1870. It's a reasonable guess that the clandestine Destroy Keble Society was already long established by the time revellers sang Auld Lang Syne to usher in 1871. As is the prerogative of secret societies, the Destroy Keble Society have been known by other scent-putting-off titles, amongst them: The Nick A Brick Society. The name itself implies an

St John's College.

objection to Keble's architectural delinquency, with frequent criticisms made of Keble's polychromatic brickwork; Magdalen student John Betjeman refused to walk past it.

Such architectural prejudices were simply transmogrified religious prejudices. For many centuries, until the formal ending of the Thirty-Nine Articles of Faith, Oxford University had repeatedly been bullied and subjugated by muscular Anglicanism, with Catholics excluded for fully 400 years. Oxford removed the mandatory religious texts for BA students in 1854. Inevitably, like a younger brother following an older brother around and copying everything he does, Cambridge applied the same rule two years later. Keble was simply disliked for its High Church Oxford Movement origins and, perhaps more controversially, an idealistic ideology offering student places to the poor.

WILDE TIMES

Oscar Wilde spent four years in Oxford, coming up to Magdalen in 1870. His public statement that nothing in life could compare to his collection of blue glass prompted a visit to his staircase from the college rugby club to teach him a decidedly non-academic lesson.

There's something inherently pleasing about the image of Wilde – man of letters though tall and physically imposing – throwing an entire rugby team down the stairs, collapsing like fifteen boisterous, boorish and bullish dominoes. It's just a pity that he only threw the rugby team down a college staircase, and that Wilde didn't inhabit rooms at the top of a lighthouse.

SHELLEY'S SHOCKING TREATMENT

Percy Shelley came up to Oxford in 1810 intent on studying chemistry as opposed to literature, and undertook research into the then fledgling science of electricity – mainly providing him with the necessary technical expertise to connect a strong electrical current to the metallic door knob of an unpopular don.

An unreconstructed prankster, Shelley would frequently be spotted tip-toeing along the High Street; whenever he saw townswomen stopping for a chat, and whilst they were distracted conversing with each other, Shelley would swap over newborn babies in their prams.

The Shelley Memorial.

Renowned for discouraging individualism, the dons had spotted Shelley as an earlier lit blot on their radar screens scanning for student nonconformity. Rebuffing the contemporary fashion of the era for short hair, Shelley wore his hair extravagantly long and uncombed. Within a few weeks of arriving at University College he had authored an incendiary pamphlet titled *The Necessity of Atheism*, which was a deliberately myopic career move in conservative 1810 Oxford.

Shelley died in a boating accident in Italy in 1822, and managed to taunt his former college both from and with the grave: his original headstone, destined for the English Ceremony in Rome, was too large to comply with regulations, so it was despatched by sea to his old college instead, where it currently resides in a purpose-built domed mausoleum – significantly a mausoleum without a body – proudly displayed in the same college that expelled him without noticeable reluctance after only two terms in Oxford. His memorial continues to be the site of student pranks dedicated to his honour as it's frequently discovered adorned in fancy dress.

SNOW MORE PUNS

Trinity students were rusticated in 1867 for blocking the passageway to chapel with a huge shovelled snow drift. Having ensured chapel could no longer be attended, they then proceeded to guarantee a nice undisturbed lie-in by cutting the bell ropes.

Snowmen at Martyrs' Memorial.

BRASSED OFF

In March 1868, University College students – now newly returned but not rehabilitated from rustication following public drunkenness – waited until an unpopular don had retired to his room for the night, and then screwed his door to the doorframe with several long brass screws. Clutching a ladder, the undergraduates proceeded to tip-toe out of the college, past a dozing porter, and into the High Street for phase two of the prank: ascending the ladder and drilling further screws to fasten the fellow's windows shut.

The next morning the trapped don hammered on his door – a door that students showed a unanimous disinclination to open. Upon discovering his windows were also sealed, he broke a pane with a shoe and, spotting the Master walking beneath his window, screamed out the ill-judged and presumably pedestrian-neck-swivelling remark: 'Help! I've been screwed!!'

University College's response was sudden and severe: they indefinitely suspended every student in the college until the culprits identified themselves. Two weeks later they did, and the Master promptly sent them down. Cunning stunt though – as New College student William Spooner probably wouldn't have said.

A similar justice tactic was deployed in the same year at New College, when in November 1868 several disliked fellows discovered that their windows had been broken. An indefinite rustication of all students until an admission of guilt was forthcoming, proved again to be a successful strategy – although the entire college was exiled for ten full days before the guilty party owned up and received his inevitable expulsion.

LODER W*NKERS

The Loder's Club, also known as Loders for King and Country Club, was an organisation populated exclusively by sons of gentry who hunted foxes. In 1870 they lobbed a stone at a library window in Christ Church and then forced entry: an act apparently motivated by the opportunity to win a bet of one guinea.

All the statues and marble busts were removed from the library, then placed in a circle in Peckwater Quad. The students then lit an enormous bonfire, which burned for several hours, destroying the majority of statues and disfiguring the rest. Multiple expulsions and rustications followed. One of the three expelled was a nobleman who arrogantly informed the college that his father would simply write a letter and he would be back after the weekend. He did write a letter; he did not return to college.

GYM BETTING SLIP

In 1825 the Chancellor of the University, Lord Grenville, vetoed the building of a gymnasium for Oxford, stating that Oxford students were highly evolved at ensuring any sporting locations were immediately turned into gambling opportunities.

Oxford did eventually receive a pioneering gymnasium and the still surviving building, opposite The Bear public house, does possess a case for being one of England's oldest purpose-built gyms, usurping the usual claimant of the title: namely the German Gym in St Pancras; would you like a bet on it being the oldest … OK, I see Lord Grenville's point.

FAIRER SEX FOR ALL

All Oxford students were male – well, just for the first 700 years of Oxford University's existence. Yet by the early 1870s there was sufficient momentum to allow women Oxford places, culminating in the delivery of that objective before the decade slammed shut. So, how far did women then progress in Oxford once they'd arrived? Surely fully integrated equality would occur speedily and naturally? Well, written almost 100 hundred years later, here's an extract from Balliol's College Rules of 1965:

> Special leave is not required for ladies entering the college only to attend lectures and tutorials. However, Ladies leaving the college between 7.30 p.m. and 11 p.m. must be accompanied by the undergraduate who has entered them [no sniggering], and he must sign his name in the book at the Lodge when they leave.

Indeed the official rules of Balliol concludes the matter with the directive: 'Ladies are not allowed in the stationery stores.'

Eventually Balliol's fellows voted 30 to 8 in favour of accepting women in the 1970s, albeit at a deliberately unspecified date, with one voting dissenter being heard to utter aloud that 'women would

Balliol College.

require full length mirrors in all the rooms'. Judging by the ramshackle appearance of numerous Oxford dons, mirrors are evidently forbidden in their college rooms to this day.

Yet women's arrival in Oxford was often an uncomfortable transition. In 1927 the Oxford Union had debated and passed a motion entitled 'The Women's colleges should be razed to the ground'. Principal Hazel of Jesus College later went on record to opine that 'women had not been treated ungenerously given how little they contributed to the University'. Clearly being called Hazel renders you a nut. Nevertheless, in spite of some liberal dissent, Congregation passed the assertion by 229 votes to 164 that 'the University retains the right to remain predominately a men's University' in 1927. Chauvinistic rhetoric soon became chauvinistic action: the colleges immediately ordered a culling of women's places, and a reductive policy was initiated, cutting the number to under 700. Cambridge issued propaganda that Oxford had become feminised, and hence this explained their students 'acting like girls' in matters of sport and academia. Beneficiaries of this sexist policy were Britain's fledgling universities, suddenly identifying a way to attract the fine female minds that Oxford and Cambridge loudly rejected, and it was Oxbridge's denunciation of women, and accommodation elsewhere by other progressive universities, that saw their traditional dominance threatened.

Eventually, the barrier fixing women students at a capped quota of 700 was abolished. Congregation minutes from the period reveal slight reasoning for the decades of being actively ostracised: a fear that women would cause pressure on the city's landladies by requiring better rooms with private toilet facilities.

Yet Oxford's female students continued to endure considerable refutation elsewhere. Henry Maudsley went on record with the following view: 'the level of study required to obtain an Oxford degree would induce brain activity likely to cause a woman to become infertile'. If you think these are the far-right fulminations of survivalists camped out in the Montana Mountains then bear in mind that Maudlesy was a highly educated individual. Furthermore, he founded the internationally recognised eponymous Maudlsey Hospital in London with his own money and acted as editor of the *British Journal of Psychiatry* for over fifty years. So we're probably going to have to reduce the charges against him and blame the times instead, and move on.

One Victorian don, Sidney Owen, objected to women's presence in Oxford on 'moral, social, physiological as well as religious grounds.' One suspects that a lot of people probably objected to Sidney Owen's presence on moral, social, physiological and religious grounds. And although views were expressed in private that there could hardly be anywhere less suitable for female inclusion that the horrendously male Oxford bubble, by the late 1870s, Owen's chauvinistic outpourings were viewed as mere contravallations amongst a besieging army of enlightenment.

Punch ran a cartoon when the first women colleges were incepted in 1878, portraying women behaving in the traditional male undergraduate manner: i.e. rioting with the townspeople.

Even as late as the mid-1930s, the women's colleges still enforced a bizarre rule that should a man visit a lady student in her room, then the bed must be wheeled out into the corridor for the duration of the visit. This would procure the anticipated effect of (a) ladies not going to the trouble of inviting gentlemen (b) doing it on all fours over a chair.

All Souls refused to relax a rule forbidding women from being in the rooms of male members of college when, in 1932, they received a written request from a fellow to host a female visitor. Permission was declined. It's probably worth pointing out that the fellow was requesting permission for a visit from … his wife. Clearly the college's visible interpretation was that those who had married had succumbed to fraternising with the enemy. Susan Hurley eventually became the first female fellow of All Souls in 1981, after a mere 543 years.

Female students were expressly forbidden from indulging in any of the following occupations: going for a walk, attending the theatre or cinema, driving, being driven, bike riding, frequenting a café without at least two other women in attendance and even then, only after receiving prior written permission from the head of college. Hence an innocent: 'would you like to go for a coffee now', would probably take a minimum of forty-eight hours to arrange, and by the time the two regulatory accompanying females had been recruited, they'd then discover one had just been sent down for leaving a table leg uncovered at lunch, or had accidentally shown a brief flash of wrist when passing the salt to a gentleman at dinner and was subsequently rusticated for such saucy displays akin to being a brazen temptress.

Just in case this practice was considered insufficiently oppressive, double-chaperoned mixed meetings in cafés were permitted only between 2 p.m. and 5.30 p.m. The University's pointed inference here suggesting that any female student out consuming tea and Dundee cake at 5.31 p.m. in a polite High Street café was practically indistinguishable from a sex worker!

HOUSE RULES

Christ Church held a meeting in the 1970s to discuss the inclusion of female students, and several fellows allegedly spoke against this unnecessary genuflection to fashionable short-termism by citing that (a) it would reduce the talent pool for the rugby team (b) women would be more likely to steal books from the library. Nevertheless, by 1980 women had been voted into Christ Church.

St Hilda's, home of Oxford's mythical Hildabeasts – think party-attending, drink-consuming, man-ruining female students expelled from St Trinian's – also suffered chauvinistic attacks, when male undergraduates responded to women's newly won right to obtain degrees in the inter-war years by sinking St Hilda's college barge when moored in the Cherwell.

Several decades later, male undergraduates returned to the banks of the River Cherwell opposite St Hilda's in an ill-fated attempt to gatecrash the girls' college ball. One chemistry student snorkelled his way to the ball – or rather, waiting security personnel – whilst a similar reception greeted a boat of male students after they had punted their way in the dark and grazed themselves sliding under barbed wire.

HORNY STUDENTS

Undergraduate partygoers were distracted from their late-night revelry one evening in 1835 when James Ingram, President of Trinity College, stormed into a student house and proceeded to smack the noisy partying undergraduates liberally around the head with a French Horn – striking a note for justice.

GOING FOR A BURTON

Explorer Richard Burton gratified his love of languages by speaking no less than twenty-six fluently, though he is perhaps best known as the Westerner who translated the *Karma Sutra* into English – a book responsible for providing more work for chiropractors than anything else.

Evidence that Richard Burton was an unapologetic snob is considerable, especially given that he described his arrival at Oxford as: 'I felt as if I had been dropped amongst greengrocers'.

During formal hall in his first week at Trinity in 1840, Burton briefly endured a fellow undergraduate teasing his moustache. Lacking a humorous personality, Burton immediately responded by challenging the student to a duel at dawn the next morning on the college lawn. His opponent demonstrated common sense by not turning up, although Burton did ... along with the college authorities. When challenged by the dons that he was there to conduct a duel, Burton became emollient and said he had only arrived to apologise and buy the other student breakfast – a defence somewhat undermined by the dons discovering a loaded pistol concealed beneath his gown. And what was his considered punishment for attempting to shoot dead a fellow student during his first week in college? Answer: a mere suspension for a fortnight – the punitive equivalent of being sent straight to bed without a second helping of chocolate pudding.

Burton did eventually get expelled from Oxford, albeit for a far more heinous crime in the eyes of the University authorities than mere murder. The story starts a little earlier, in 1833, when Isambard Kingdom Brunel was commissioned to build the Great Western Railway linking London to Bristol; Oxford, being approximately the halfway point, was earmarked to become a significant railway town, providing rival employment for townspeople with the University. The plan never reached fruition after the Chancellor of Oxford University, the Duke of Wellington, furiously fulminated: 'we do not want the railway coming to Oxford as it will merely encourage the lower orders to move around'. And they say that Oxford's elitist?!

When the railway did eventually arrive in Oxford, it was forbidden by a practised by-law installed by the University from selling tickets to any destination with a horseracing course, as they believed this would discourage students from gambling. Hence Richard Burton saw a business opportunity, and ran stagecoach trips departing from Trinity College to Ascot – until the dons discovered his illicit industry and promptly sent him down.

His arrival in Oxford was exuberant, and he ensured his departure matched. Leaving Oxford for the final time involved his carriage deliberately circling across the college flowerbeds, then proceeding along the High Street blowing a large trumpet (probably not the first time Burton was observed blowing his own trumpet in Oxford), whilst stopping intermittently to kiss bemused shop girls. The scale of Burton's unsurpassable ego in life can be comparatively measured in death by the size of his ostentatious memorial in St Mary Magdalene, Mortlake.

CHAMBER MUSIC

Mass expulsions occurred in 1890 when the University authorities decided to adopt a tough approach to drunkenness. The wonderfully named Baron von Zedlitz was sent down that year for being so drunk that he was discovered by the proctors attempting to swim back to college along the Broad Street pavement.

Four years later, undergraduate Alan Lascelles was sent down for stringing a line of chamber pots across his college's quadrangle, and encouraging other students to hammer them with wooden spoons – though on the plus size, he was probably rewarded with a Turner Prize nomination.

BATH NIGHT

Guy Fawkes Night had become renowned for Town and Gown violence well before the nineteenth century and both townspeople and students would eagerly enter into their diaries for 5 November: 'RIOT!!!' Oxford's council and colleges would provide free fireworks events as distractions to discourage rioting, yet this often resulted in only partial success. Violence frequently occurred and on the evening of 5 November 1892 the long-standing bonfire night rioting tradition was upheld when the townspeople threw a bath through a window at Exeter College – quite a logistical effort on the part of the townspeople, dragging an iron bath along Turl Street for the purposes of hurling it through a college window; there must have been someone at the planning stage arguing that chucking a brick instead would render the logistics so much easier, plus they'd still be able to have a bath when they got back.

BERTIE WORCESTER

According to the records of Jesus College, in 1811 their sozzled students sank 1,470 bottles of port, 171 of sherry and 48 of Madeira. But this is practically temperance compared to Worcester College's students of the era, who habitually sconced each another. 'Sconcing' is the Oxford tradition of downing a glass trumpet of ale, usually containing approximately 2.5 pints. A Worcester student named Bertie, recurrently sconced 'for being boring at dinner', requested that the ale was substituted for whisky. He then consumed 2.5 pints of single malt in roughly thirty seconds. He was discovered dead in his room the next morning – what a lightweight!

SUPER BOWL

Jesus College possess a striking eighteenth-century silver punch bowl. The bowl was taken to the Radcliffe Camera in 1814 where the Duke of Wellington, the Tsar of Russia and the King of Prussia collectively toasted Napoleon's recent defeat to their armies. A long-standing college tradition decrees that any student or visitor can possess the silver bowl by performing just two challenges: (a) wrap their arms around the bowl (probably ought to mention that it measures over 5ft in diameter) and (b) down the entire alcoholic content of the bowl in one (also probably need to point out that it holds ten gallons). Still, if anyone can succeed in winning the priceless bowl, then it would have to be students: after all, many in Oxford seem to be in permanent training for the second stage of this challenge.

ARMCHAIR SPORTS FAN

Whereas Oxford's academic community in the 1860s ought to have been obsessed with the breaking ideas of the age such as Darwinism, undergraduates were instead reportedly obsessed with the proclaimed student innovation of the era: chair tilting. This was basically improvised dodgems, only with armchairs since, frustratingly, dodgems hadn't been invented yet. Undergraduates would sit back-to-back in armchairs in the centre of a college quad, and then attempt to topple their competitor's chair, or push them to the edge of the quadrangle arena – the first student to succeed with either action was proclaimed the game's winner. Each college champion would then go on to represent their esteemed academic institution against a rival college. Bizarre as this sounds, this self-invented sport apparently gripped Oxford undergraduate life for over a decade.

YOU SEE HELL

Jeremy Bentham came up to Queen's College aged twelve, departing three years later with the pernicious parting shot: 'mendacity and insincerity I have found to be the only sure effects of an English university education' before becoming the spiritual founder of University College London (UCL) in 1826.

NEW DIRECTION

In the late nineteenth century, New College eventually renounced its peculiar lone privilege, held since the college's inception in the fourteenth century, of handing out degrees to students without the requirement to sit any troubling examinations. Once rescinded, New College's academic reputation flowered; and it needed to, given that Anthony Wood had once referenced it as 'a stinking pile of ruinous waste, with drinking, gaming, whoring and cockfighting whilst only one member remains sober' (which as Ofsted reports go, isn't a great one).

Oxford's Sherriff and Lord Mayor ritually inspect the city wall at New College.

EIGHT

THE TWENTIETH CENTURY

Many continue to hold an illogical and lazy prejudice that contemporary Oxford is still stubbornly stuck somewhere in the 1930s.

Sketching a long lost Oxford redolent of 1930s excess, novelist Angus Wilson typifies this obsolete image that many non-Oxonians continue to willingly embrace. Wilson's initial attempt to come up to Merton ended with a prompt rejection immediately after his interview. Hence, the second option was deployed: mummy's cheque book. This provided a place, along with adequately capacious rooms above the JCR, where Wilson had to tolerate the excessive noise of upper-class students routinely 'roasting' one another (in Oxford student parlance this means forcibly submitting a victim to radiator torture – typically harmful boys-will-be-bastards stuff).

In his essay *My Oxford*, Wilson describes college food as the nadir of dining experiences, and stubbornly dined out EVERY night at Oxford's most expensive restaurant 'elaborately consuming Sole Mornay and Meringue Chantily'. He then courted a manipulative 'friendship' with the college's head chef, in order to provide luncheon parties in his rooms, and daily smoked fifty hugely expensive specially imported Turkish cigarettes through a lengthy cigarette holder that would eject the smoked stubs via pressing a button.

And yet Wilson complains that he voluntarily spent considerable time alone in Oxford, as the place was packed with pompous upper-class snobs. Surely that's a case of the snob calling the kettle a snob? Well, it shines a torch into the murky areas of Oxford's outlandish elitism, a time that we can now only light via distorting television drama productions, filtered through contemporary perceptions. Wilson may have belatedly received the ultimate accolade of establishment (i.e. a knighthood), his writing displayed a healthy liberalism; he went on to teach successfully not at Oxford or Cambridge, but in Norwich, where he instigated a creative writing course that wielded direct influence over a generation of writers devoid of Oxbridge pretensions such as Ian McEwan.

If Wilson's entry into Oxford was hardly textbook (i.e. he used money rather than textbooks to obtain a coveted Oxford pace), then celebrated writer, lawyer and sire of impossibly beautiful actresses – i.e. John Mortimer – was downright venal. Mortimer was responsible for a particularly successful student jape. Plus he had the added advantage of executing the prank on his first ever visit to an Oxford College.

Summoned to Brasenose for an interview along with a similarly hopeful friend, Mortimer was met by a disinterested bald don with a protruding nose and features resembling a bird of prey. Handing Mortimer and friend a large slab of Latin text, he ordered them into separate rooms to translate it, prior to finding him in the college dinning hall when the translation task had been completed.

Upon the immediate discovery that the Latin prose was impenetrably difficult, Mortimer resigned himself to an education elsewhere. A knock on the door caused Mortimer to assume that the don had returned to collect his feeble attempt at translation, but discovered his friend beaming confidently on the staircase, for he had discovered Blackwell's bookshop within a three-minute walk of Brasenose, and emptied a paper bag onto the desk containing two English/Latin dictionaries. Well, as Jean Paul Sartre once proposed, cheating is just another way of playing.

The 1930s may still be adopted as a template for contemporary Oxford by many of its visitors, yet Mortimer, in a departure from his customary avuncular style of memoir, realised it was changing by the 1940s, even though he was castigating towards the elements of snobbery he encountered in wartime Oxford.

Student misbehaviour continued to revolve around consuming heroic quantities of alcohol, and Mortimer had a penchant for brandy and dry sherry mixed together and boiled in an electric kettle.

Most Oxford undergraduates of the time report associations with dons who were career alcoholics; one such unfortunate don, responsible for hours of tedious lectures instilling a knowledge of Roman Law into his undergraduates (as Mortimer himself once observed: 'I've never found it to be of great service in Uxbridge Magistrates Court'), discovered the combination of short-slightness and alcohol to be fatal one evening, when returning from a drinks party in London and mistaking the train door for a toilet door when passing at speed through Didcot.

RUNNING WITH THE BULLERS

Student drinking culture remained dominant, and Oxford institutionalised alcoholism by forming various dining societies – 'dining' omits the crucial 'r' and 'k' required to form the word 'drinking', but its *raison d'etre* is hardly disguised by a couple of missing consonants.

Oxford's d(r)in(k)ing clubs are often exclusive: and exclusivity is undeniably the attraction here. The Bullingdon Club is perhaps the most well known, yet at times the rival Piers Gaverston Society make the Bullingdon look restrained. Membership is strictly imposed to only twelve students. Adopting their name from King Edward II's catamite (Edward II died by having a red-hot poker shoved up … like you require me to finish this sentence!), members are usually responsible for making more noise than the unfortunate king managed during his final evening. Although members sometimes elect to wear drag, their appetite for decadence is permanent whenever convened at a clandestine location. Suggestions have been made that former members indulged in champagne, drugs and caviar inspired orgies, and a level of debauchery that would have seen Lord Byron storming out in disgust.

Alleged former members, whom we're sure behaved impeccably if they ever were in the PGS, include a descendant of Otto von Bismarck and former New College student and Hollywood actor Hugh Grant.

WAUGH DAMAGE

The Bullingdon feature in Evelyn Waugh's *Decline and Fall*. Waugh scraped a lower Third degree, after coming up to Hertford College in 1922. A scene referring to a fictional college summoning the best port from the cellar whenever a student had been fined £50 by the dons was said to have been based on Waugh's own multiple indiscretions.

BULLY BOYS

The Bullingdon operates with a clandestine code, strictly discouraging members to discuss their antics (well, apart from in multiple newspapers, magazines, books and a 2009 Channel Four documentary, anyway). One member quickly regretted using a portaloo during one of the club's 1993 events, when a revolving sensation alerted him to fact that he was being rolled down a hillside by his fellow Bullers.

Several highly successful lawyers were members of the Bully, so the next paragraph may have incurred some edits prior to publication:

> Restaurant ... hotel ... two prostitutes ... pints of champagne ... brandy ... broken window at St Clements ... police chase ... Oxford's Botanical Garden ... very sore bottom ... successful politician.

In the late 1980s open-top buses were hired, along with members of professions that don't tend to pay income tax. Venues are booked under assumed names, though the Old Bear at Woodstock is rumoured to have received the traditional cheque for damages. Still, it's not as if any of the Bullingdon Club are going to end up running the country, is it?

KCC — FINGER LICKING BAD

Perhaps no other student dining society managed to combine riotous vandalism while simultaneously aspiring to high royalist standards better than the King Charles Club. Founded at St John's College, their minute books note disapprovingly that a member once used his fingers to consume some food at dinner (a coarse course indeed), yet is highly supportive of that same member later hurling wine glasses at ancient college statues. The King Charles Club (KCC) existed to mark the anniversary of Charles I losing his head — Britain's shortest monarch, even before he lost his head.

Indeed, members of KCC routinely disregarded both statues and statutes. The college amended their written regulations to insert a clause ensuring that the KCC became a banned organisation, though they continued to resurface occasionally in a strictly subterranean capacity. Statue abuse was also part of the club's *raison d'etre*, and the wonderfully decorous Canterbury Quad would host the annual 29 January regicide anniversary with King Charles' statue being pelted with glasses and bottles. Inevitably such abuse of the college's prized seventeenth-century statue could not be permitted to continue. Although another essential part of the ceremony — namely Dean baiting — did proceed.

The minutes of 1955 recall:

> Members of the club met to commemorate the martyrdom of King Charles I. After sufficient mulled claret had been imbibed to lull caution without arousing folly, a procession was formed and a wake solemnly conducted throughout the quads of the college to the sounds of keening to gongs, cymbals and a voice crying through a mighty trumpet 'woe woe woe the king is dead'. The procession concluded without the Dean rising to this annually offered bait.

Members were aware of their need to tone down the processional wailing 'mainly out of consideration for visitors whose sartorial magnificence has thereby been spoilt in the past'. The minutes also record complaints that the invited guests were often 'old and dull', and hence invitations were sent out to invite the young and fascinating … well, Harold MacMillan. He declined. As did an astonishing array of invitees, their invitations displaying an arrogant confidence in an Oxford student's self-important hubris: John Betjeman, J.R.R. Tolkien, Peter Sellers, Ian Fleming and the Prince of Wales all politely (and occasionally impolitely) declined.

By the mid-1960s times were hard as the country lurched towards recession. While the nation prepared to cut an extra hole in their belt to allow additional tightening, Wilson's government pledged the country would require forbearance. Clearly anxious to show that the KCC, no doubt aware they represented the public's perceived Oxford privilege, were prepared to make their own selfless empathetic sacrifice for the country's economic struggle: in 1965 they took the decision to reduce their dinner from eight courses to seven. Like Wilson's premiership, their time was running out and they were looking increasingly anachronistic as the 1970s moved towards a close.

Charles I statue in St John's.

Although the invitees were declining, the quantities of consumed claret and riotous behaviour were increasing:

> ... with the force of the truly impassioned, sixty glasses projected with similar force by fellow mourners, one of which, the aim of whose owner may perhaps have been blurred by tears, fractured a library window. At this stage the penitents indulged in mortification of the flesh by discharging fire extinguishers among themselves, encouraging other members of the college to join them by attempting to include all those visible in the absolved spray. They also showed their taste for modern civilised methods by scattering roles of lavatory paper on the cool wind, by breaking large numbers of bottles on college buildings and destroying notices not to walk on the grass.

This is behaviour that Bertie Wooster would consider unnecessarily decadent.

The next morning the Junior Dean used a ladder to carry out a damage inspection. Inevitably the KCC committee members were dragged in front of the President, only to complain irascibly in the subsequent minutes that 'the President, Secretary and Junior Dean treated us like recalcitrant prep-school boys'.

That was pretty much it for the recalcitrant prep-school boys as the KCC was forced into official disbandment by the St John's authorities. They became active again whenever bans expired, though a proclivity for chair tossing through college windows ensured further interdiction, even regenerating intermittently in the 1980s and '90s – the last occasion culminating in a visit from the fire brigade and a crude attempt to build a wall partitioning the North Quad. If they've reincarnated again, then no one is saying.

The other notorious St John's dining club was the Archery Club, which included former St John's law student and lead singer of the college's rock band Ugly Rumours, Tony Blair as a member. Blair was photographed in the St John's garden with fellow club members making an obscene gesture – a hand movement subsequently airbrushed out of the commonly circulating version, until BBC's *Newsnight* displayed the original photo with restored vulgarity in 2007.

SEE YOU LATER, ALLIGATOR

Other eccentric clubs were also coming to an end in the twentieth century. The Crocodile Club was founded in 1896, and Brasenose College retains the club's initial rules, handwritten by *The 39 Steps* author John Buchan.

The first rule of the Crocodile Club is … there are many rules of Crocodile Club: for example 'that no one be eligible for membership who has any serious stain on his moral character i.e. who is either a Baptist, an Anabaptist, a Socialist, a Whig, a 'blood', a 'weird pard', or a' gentleman who parts his hair in the middle.' The minutes of an early meeting called for the college's President to change his title to 'Dictator'.

Oh and another rule, just obvious formal bureaucratic administration, stated that all meetings of the club had to be conducted in the presence of a real crocodile. Fortuitously, there was a stuffed crocodile belonging to one of the students and since he kept the specimen in his college rooms (demonstrating the typical student approach to only packing the essentials when coming up to Oxford for a term) the club was inaugurated.

By 1921 pedants had pointed out it was probably an alligator and hence the club was permanently discontinued until an actual crocodile could be sourced.

RISE OF THE PHOENIX

Brasenose also supplied one of Oxford University's oldest established dining groups, known as the Phoenix Club. Given that the Phoenix held their centenary dinner in 1886, and celebrated their bicentenary in 1982, this was clearly not a club favoured by maths students. The society's counting abilities were probably affected by the college ruling in 1795 that the club's twelve members were not allowed to consume more than thirty-six bottles of port and sherry a week – well, to a student that's practically prohibition!

The Phoenix Club was restricted to merely twelve members attired in mandatory claret suits (presumably chosen to hide wine stains), though college records reveal that some members would dress in Turkish trousers mismatched with floral-patterned velvet waistcoats. Four unfortunate student members were expelled in 1844: not for crimes against fashion, but for playing cards on a Sunday.

REACHING THE ZENITH

The ultimate dining club is probably the Zeniths, founded in 1902. Their inaugural dinner descended into a drunken Town and Gown scrap, followed by a mass brawl between fellow Zenith members, leaving a trail of destroyed property. Chased by the proctors across Oxford, the Zeniths then commenced their third fight with their third separate enemy of the evening: the University's own proctors. Every member of the club was fined and promptly sent down from Oxford. Which gives them a unique status amongst Oxford dining societies, as the Zenith record reads: one dinner, ten members, ten permanent expulsions.

LET THE TORY BEGIN

Of course, not every Oxford student migrates towards d(r)in(k)ing societies and connected carnage. There is also a category of student that spend their three years as an undergraduate behaving impeccably with boring impunity to subsequent embarrassing student revelations. Former Oxford students in this category include Margaret Thatcher – described by her own chemistry tutor at Somerville College as someone 'who one day will make a perfectly good second-rate chemist'. Her tutor at Somerville, and the unlikely verbal sniper who orated the remark, was none other than Nobel Prize winning scientist Dorothy Hodgkin – whose parents sentenced her to a school life of name-calling when christening her with the unfortunate middle name Crowfoot.

This prophecy failed to accurately materialise as Oxford sparked her political interest, and she enrolled in the Oxford University Conservative Association in 1944. The OUCA is an entry route into politics for those who consider the Oxford Union to be a militant far-left workers' collective.

Former members include William Hague, Edward Heath and Ed Balls (the latter being decidedly odd, given he became a member of the Labour cabinet and recipient of the parliamentary heckle 'that's not Brown, that's Balls').

According to the *Independent*, an Oxford rugby team were ordered by the proctors to attend a diversity training session after circulating a dinner invitation containing the directive:'bring a fit Jew'.Yet a crasser display of cultural insensitivity occurred in 2009, when an OUCA hustings for the presidency culminated in two members allegedly attempting to tell the most racist joke, with the *Oxford Mail* reporting 'proctors have ruled that the OUCA can no longer use the name of Oxford University' or, as they're presumably now called, the CA.

Oxford's longstanding student newspaper *The Cherwell* initiated an annual Pushy Fresher Award in the 1970s, and subsequent winners included BBC political correspondent Nick Robinson, who was also a member of the OUCA.

Another winner was William Hague. One evening, a group of medical students were making their way along the High Street to attend a party when they spotted Hague, whose notorious 1977 Toryboy conference speech had rendered him both recognisable and slapable for a generation. The medical students instantly recognised Hague, and allegedly debagged him.

William Hague then appeared at the party, seeking to encounter the group again. Hague was known as a dogged political fighter, this being quite different from being an actual fighter, and since he was outnumbered approximately six to one, he would probably be beaten as easily as Michael Howard at a general election. Hague angrily rang the doorbell.When the ring-leader of the medical students opened the door, it's alleged that Hague delivered a fight-winning single punch on the chief bully.

Yet Hague, who once famously told a journalist that he had regularly consumed fourteen pints in an evening, is primarily remembered in Oxford for energetically ensuring that the Oxford Union bar stocked a more expansive range of real ales.

Other famous political party aspirants who had set up political base camp whilst at Oxford include Michael Heseltine.When a student at Pembroke College he charted his political career on a menu in the JCR one evening, and kept that power route map with him over the passing decades, excitedly ticking off each stage reached – well, apart from the final stage, unless he had prophesied all those years earlier:'will lose

Tory party leadership election to bloke who only had three O Levels and didn't go to University'.

HUGH'S GRANT

Women's college St Hugh's started in a semi-detached house founded by a relative of William Wordsworth. In what was presumably an attempt to prove that St Hugh's natural twin is St Trinian's, the girls once barricaded an unpopular Principal in the toilet. When the head of college finally managed to escape, she retaliated by withdrawing a grant earmarked for that year's anticipated college ball. The fact that the main perpetrator was identified as the daughter of an earl ensured that the *Daily Mail* became involved, and the miscreant female was re-instated – although the ball wasn't.

Women were exempted from wearing academic dress when out in the town until 1959, which enabled them to be unrecognisable as students – conveniently ensuring that proctors could not easily identify them. Somerville's records reveal that one student obtained a First Class degree in 1935 in spite of a noted proclivity for drunkenness, attending balls rather than lectures, and a penchant for bedding clergymen.

NICE DREAM CONE

There's a (ig)noble student tradition of coning that is not exclusively confined to Oxford. Stroll along the streets of any University town and spot an impromptu traffic cone hat adorning a statue, and you are guaranteed to be within close proximity to the university.

Given the size of Oxford's transient student population, traffic cones are much coveted.

Traffic cones have an inflated black-market value, not unlike tobacco in prisons. Luckily for students, the city is constantly being dug upon by perpetual cyclical road works, so cones are usually in abundant supply.

Whereas most conings are relatively unimaginative exercises, with individual cones predictably placed with a tedious frequency upon phone-boxes and bus shelters, there are occasional flashes of pioneering coning genius. Entering into the coning hall of fame is Nicholas Troen, who attended St Catherine's College. He is the coner who dismantled the restraining barriers of conventional coning wisdom, and re-erected them several metres further forward – he is The Beatles, the Charles Darwin and the Picasso of coning, one man's vision leading to advancement in their chosen art form that others couldn't imagine until it had already happened.

In the late Noughties, during Nicholas's first term in Oxford, he devoted himself to hatching an epic scheme. Like Alexander Graham Bell before him, who was ridiculed for suggesting that people could one

St Catherine's College.

day speak to someone miles away simply by using electrical signals in a wire, Nicholas remained unflinchingly focused on his dream. And one night before Christmas, the planning achieved fruition. For Nicholas had successfully coned every one of the Emperors' Heads that necklace the Sheldonian Theatre. As Nicholas himself remarked, like a proud goal scorer during the post-match interview: 'This is what made my first Michaelmas in Oxford: coning every single head of busts outside the Sheldonian. I know it seems childish, but it's the kind of thing that brings freshers together. We spent a week planning the whole thing and gathering cones from around Oxford.' This was coning on a hitherto unrealised scale.

DOUBTING THOMAS ABILITY

When news reached Britain that the strategic Boar War siege of Mafeking had been relieved in 1900, prompting national rejoicing, Lincoln College student Edward Thomas was moved to emphasise the seemingly willing apartheid between Town and Gown demonstrated in Oxford during the country's celebrations. He wrote in a letter, now held in a Cardiff archive:

> The whole of the City and University were in the streets. On such occasions the city acknowledges its inferiority. All the women married or otherwise, allow themselves to be promiscuously kissed by the University students. In fact most men employed themselves in recording as many kisses as possible. Nearly everyone was drunk, except the citizens, who looked on with the utmost complacence.

Thomas admits in his letter that 'two of whom brought me home when, after an excited evening, I succumbed to the wine I had taken. For universal good temper you never saw such a night. Although all were very ill and cheap the next morning, few regretted it.'

Hence Edward Thomas boasts, in the dignifying euphemisms of the age, that he participated in a threesome with two Town girls.

The problem here being ... Thomas chose to compose these words of revelation in a letter to his wife Helen. Subsequently Thomas contracted a venereal disease from the encounter that impacted upon his Finals, to the extent that he narrowly avoided barrel-scraping a lowly Third Class degree.

Impish behaviour at Lincoln College.

INSPECTOR LEWIS

Wadham undergraduate Cecil Day-Lewis was sufficiently aggravated by his college's staffing standards to include the somewhat pernicious description of Oxford's scouts in his 1938 work *Anatomy of Oxford*: 'A more rascally set of human beings cannot be imagined as they are generally a dirty, idle, thievish, impudent set'. He goes on to expose that routine student behaviour of the age ensured breakfast was accompanied by two cups: one for beer and one for cider, before stating that the average college scout's idea of dinner is three desserts and ten glasses of wine. Although there was certainly rumour of more than just cigar smoke permeating some junior, middle and senior common rooms during this era.

ER

Oxford proudly lays claim to numerous world-improving inventions. Penicillin understandably tends to grab the headlines, yet another Dreaming Spires invention was the tradition of bolting 'er' onto the end of nouns. This was an infectious fashion in the 1920s/30s, and many of these Oxford student creations have survived importation into daily English usage ... fiver, rugger, skiver, cuppers, preggers, tenner.

Students were creatively employed in Oxford's history inventing nicknames for seemingly everything and everyone: Merton student Richard Swineshead, who became a fellow of his college in 1344, rejoiced in the nickname The Calculator (presumably he only worked in sunlight, and said 'bollocks' whenever he was turned upside down).

WRITING'S ON THE WALL

Christ Church awoke one morning in 1911 to discover the words 'Bloody Dean' crudely dawbed on a wall in white paint. The culprit, although readily named by several witnesses, originally denied his involvement in the incident – until the Dean interviewing him in his office, pointed to the undergraduate's boots and hands that were smeared in the same shade of white paint deployed to disabuse the Dean. Caught white-handed, an inevitable expulsion (or should that be emulsion?) followed.

UNHOLY TRINITY

Students from an ethnic background were rare in Oxford until the beginning of the twentieth century, when Balliol started to receive members of the Indian Civil Service. Certainly they were racially unenlightened times, and in 1914 the Dean fined Trinity student Thomas Cathrall for altering a newspaper seller's board from 'Negros Riot in Cardiff' to 'Negros Riot in Balliol'.

Showing their political leanings, Oxford undergraduates travelled to Hull during the 1926 General Strike to act as strike breakers, and drove tams. Soon the students' tribal loyalties leaked into their new roles, and trams were adorned in colours representing their colleges, ending with Balliol and Trinity's trams deliberately ramming and bumping each other, as if transplanted back to the Isis in Eights Week.

Meanwhile several New College students, representing a dining club renowned for possessing some unpalatable politics, targeted one of Oxford's leading public supporters of the General Strike; having ambushed him in Broad Street, he was forced to sing God Save the King, prior to being debagged and left to waddle back to college like a penguin.

Balliol's drive towards cosmopolitan modernity enabled them to portray their rival Trinity as xenophobic – a prejudice that doesn't necessarily stand up to historical examination given that Balliol's offensive song about Trinity is named after Gordouli who was a foreign student himself.

Gordouli had the misfortune to occupy rooms that overlooked Balliol when he came up to Trinity in 1894. Indeed, his actual name –

Galetti-di-Cadilhac – was corrupted by students unable or unwilling to properly pronounce his name, and hence called him Gordouli after a popular cigarette brand. Faced with a daily torrent of abuse and pebbles from the Balliol students outside his window, he unsurprisingly retaliated with a few choice words and pebbles of his own.

The tradition of Balliol students gathering on the last day of Michaelmas term, marching to the gates of Trinity in Broad Street, and then delivering a heartily renditioned verse or three of the Gordouli song (the more publishable lines include the chorus refrain 'Bloody Trinity, Bloody Trinity') has been a long-standing Oxford tradition continuing into the twenty-first century.

In a retaliatory gesture, Trinity students once broke into Balliol's college bar and turfed it; Balliol responded, retaining the domesticated animal theme, by throwing numerous chickens over the wall into Trinity.

During the late 1940s Balliol suffered the humiliation of having students from next door's rival climb into the Master's bedroom in Broad Street and wake both him and his wife, prior to ascending back down the ladder.

LAUNCH MENU

Corpus fellows pinned the following decree to the college noticeboard in 1928: 'During formal hall, the fellows dining at Top Table consider it insulting to be struck, and undignified to attempt to deflect, breadstick missiles'.

Another genuine notice from the dining hall of an Oxford College between the wars read:

> Gentlemen coming from homes where bread throwing at the dinner table is habitual and finding difficulty in conforming suddenly to the unfamiliar ways of a higher civilization will be permitted to continue this domestic pastime on a payment of 5 shillings a throw during their first year. After that the charge will be doubled.

Food throwing, even attached to punitive tariffs, remains fatally tempting to students today. There remained one particular Indian restaurant in Oxford for many decades that was almost wholly reliant on a student clientele, where the served food was selected not for its culinary expertise, but purely for its aerodynamic qualities.

FREUDIAN SLIP

One of the more ambitious Oxford student hoaxes executed in the twentieth century involved an undergraduate called Mabbott placing posters around town advertising a lecture by none other than Sigmund Freud that evening. The short-notice announcement didn't deter a large expectant audience from converging at the University's museum. Hidden behind heavy makeup, and an even heavier German accent, Mabbott approached the lectern with considerable applause and trepidation. Unfortunately, he hadn't prepared a lecture, so the ruse was discovered almost immediately and it's probably fair to report that his audience did not take the prank with the good humour that he had probably anticipated in the planning stage: several burly members of the audience chased him and delivered a good beating. His attempts at Freudian psychoanalytical humour proved that, when it comes to doing couch gags, best leave it to The Simpsons.

TIME TRAVELLERS

Whenever you arrive slightly late for a tutorial and a querulous don asks, 'what time do you call this?', why not answer 'GMT'? Unless you're being asked between late March and the end of October, in which case

'BST' would be a more apt response. Reminding us when British Summer Time ends is the quaint Merton tradition of the Time Ceremony. This is an ancient Oxford student tradition, that some say harks back to the 1970s. When BST officially ends at 2 a.m. on a late October Sunday morning, Merton students attempt to reverse the previously considered irreversible passage of time by walking backwards around the quad for an hour. But that would be too easily accomplishable in itself, so in classic *It's-a-Knockout* style, participating students must down a glass of port every time they complete a few laps.

A DEAD BRILL IDEA

During an unfeasibly warm Trinity term, two students from Wadham bought a bag of fish from the Covered Market and then deliberately left it out in the strong afternoon sun. That evening, they posted the rotting fish into as many post boxes as they could find – thus causing

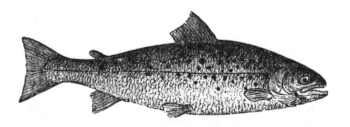

quite a stink with the Post Office and college authorities. (For cod's sake, haddock up to here with students: not a dead brill idea; college's sole responsibility to mackerel difference and hake it up to the Post Office.)

Whereas the dead fish pranksters deserved their fines, undoubtedly some students suffered unfairly at the hands of tyrannical college authorities – especially as dons had to make up their salaries with student fines. A Corpus Christi student was once fined by the President 'for looking interested and wistful at a passing beauty.'

MAKING A SPLASH

Many looked wistfully at St Hilda's student and alpha Hildabeast Jocelyn Witchard in 1995, when she appeared naked in national newspapers following the traditional May Day Morning student plunge from Magdalen Bridge into the River Cherwell below. The next day she received a phone call at college from the *Sun*, offering £1,000 for a Page Three photo shoot. Pocketing £1k for a few minutes work was understandably preferable to the traditional student jobs such as advertising poster/golf sales by wearing a sandwich board: the plywood poncho. Thus Jocelyn appeared on Page Three, receiving in her college pigeonhole soon afterwards a cheque for £1,000 – and a summons to see the college authorities. The latter's puritanism ensured Jocelyn had ended up in very deep water – which was ironic, given the Cherwell is notoriously shallow for jumping.

The problem was that Jocelyn had worn her academic mortar board hat during the Page Three shoot. And in Oxford it's always the small print that gets you. Actively disregarding the small print, preferring to focus on their customary enormous font-sized headline, the *Sun* bannered Jocelyn's photo with the huge headline: 'Girl from St Thrillda's'.

The University, burnt by the intense media glare, decided firm action was required for bringing the University into disrepute. As any Oxford pedant knows: it is unlawful for a student to wear their cap unless they have gained a degree. Hence the authorities had a reason to discipline her: for wearing her University hat in public – which was considerably ironic, given that was almost all she was wearing in the photo.

Jocelyn may have made a big splash in both the *Sun* and the River Cherwell, but her Oxford student life was now struggling to stay afloat. Her essential scholarship was likely to be removed unless she conformed to specific criteria. She begrudgingly agreed to discontinue future media activity, forced to decline further lucrative photo shoots, and wrote a formal letter of apology to the Principal.

She told the *Observer* eight years after the event: 'I felt like a princess all summer', but 'the college authorities were really angry about the publicity … the article was about what a wild place St Hilda's was, where girls partied and tore their clothes off at the slightest opportunity.'

NINE

THE TWENTY-FIRST CENTURY

Throughout the centuries, being permanently plastered off their acned faces appears to have been a demanded right of passage for a sizable cross-section of Oxford's students, endorsed by a 2010 survey that proclaimed over 70 per cent routinely drank too much whilst studying in the Dreaming Spires. One former undergraduate, who came up to University College, recounts being pressured by peers into consuming countless pints of lager, each containing a different spirit delivered in a shot glass dropped inside the pint (known as a 'depth charge'). His next conscious experience occurred fully ten hours later, when he awoke naked and encircled by his own vomit. Needless to say, he had to leave a large tip for the scouts that day.

Subsequently vowing to drink in strictly applied moderation from that day onwards, he reports that several of the previous night's participants dutifully reconvened at the bar the next evening to repeat the same drinking games.

In the same era the student beer cellar at University College offered a drink advertised as a 'Mindfuck'. One night a female student downed a Mindfuck, and declared immediately afterwards that 'it's had no effect on me 'cos, like, I can so totally take my drink, see'. Twenty minutes later four people (one allocated to each limb) carried her prostrate and insentient body out of the bar.

UNICYCLE DASH

The Turl Street Dash flourished in the Noughties after being supposedly founded by a student in 1996. Celebrated annually, the Turl Street Dash is a cycle race involving Exeter and Jesus (the Colleges – not the south western city against the Messiah). Usually, given the proximity and simmering rivalry between Jesus and Exeter, trouble inevitably occurs, and Turl Street is not a location to visit whilst the annual Dash is taking place – unless you are an ambulance crew.

In 2009 rival Jesus and Exeter students attempted to break into each other's colleges and urinate in the quad; this courted a musical

Jesus College.

Snowman in Exeter College, complete with mortar board.

response from Jesus undergraduates who loudly chorused 'Always piss on the Exeter side of the street' to the adopted tune of Monty Python's 'Always Look on the Bright Side of Life'. Both student bars emptied, as eager reinforcements scrambled to join in the ruck. Although witnesses reported that bloodstained faces and clothing were ubiquitous, a fresher told the Cherwell afterwards that 'the whole thing has been blown out of proportion, and no one deserves to be rusticated for it' – although his comments were probably rendered inaudible by the sound of body-bags being zipped up. Unsurprisingly, the event was banned the following year.

In the 1960s Exeter students acquired several pigeons, and before releasing them in Jesus' main hall, mixed their bird feed with laxatives.

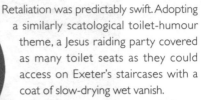

Retaliation was predictably swift. Adopting a similarly scatological toilet-humour theme, a Jesus raiding party covered as many toilet seats as they could access on Exeter's staircases with a coat of slow-drying wet vanish.

Turl Street is even named after a Town and Gown riot, when a twirl (corrupted to 'turl') gate was installed to provide an escape option after outnumbered students had been regularly trapped by townspeople in what was then a cul-de-sac following organised violence; the gate was removed from the street in 1772, but significantly not the name or violence.

FOXY WADHAM GIRLS

Wadham College originated the fine partying traditions of Queer Bop and Wadstock. Although owning a lesser profile, Wadham is also rumoured to be behind the engagingly surreal sight of townspeople occasionally spotting undergraduate females in city centre pubs supporting large whiskers, pointed ears, bushy tails and a tendency to say 'boom, boom!' after someone has made a funny. And this spectacle retains the capacity to become even weirder, whenever several male undergraduates enter the pub shortly after the bushy-tailed and blurry-eyed girls have departed – if the females have got their timing correct – attired in red coats and riding hats, whilst holding whips and hunting horns.

This is the tradition of female undergraduates dressing up as foxes, and after benefiting from a deliberately staggered start, downing one mandatory drink in every pub on an agreed route, ahead of the male undergraduates pursuing them, who must also abide by the requirement to sink a drink in each visited inn. Should the riders/hounds catch up with any straggling vixens on route, then forfeits

– supposedly of the filthy lovin' carpet-staining variety – can allegedly be demanded. Although if I were one of the pursued girls about to be caught by a randy drunken undergrad hound, I'd ensure I had a mate along pretending to be a hunt sabbaeuteur who could spray the guys off the scent. But no animals get hurt in this creative variant of blood sports and it raises money for charity, so what's not to like?

THE EMPEROR'S NEW CONES

Painting the lips of the Emperors' Heads bright fuchsia pink may have ensured an appearance on the BBC 2 flagship arts programme *The Culture Show* in 2010, where they were held up as an example of student insurrection. In reality, they were painted pink to mark a breast cancer charity! This was another example of a long-standing and continuously unfurling student tradition – the Emperors' Heads have been coloured many times to reflect contemporary events: in 1918 their faces were painted by students to celebrate Armistice Day.

Frustratingly, no one knows who the Emperors are meant to represent. Although they featured in Christopher Wren's original specifications for the Sheldonian, they were added a few years after the building's completion. Disappointingly, the current third set of heads dates from the 1970s, although the previous incumbents had deteriorated to such an egregious decline that Magdalen student John Benjamin was prompted to compare them to illustrations of skin diseases in a medical textbook.

Legend decrees that on foggy ethereal nights, the Emperors descend from their plinths and partake of a pint in the nearby White Horse public house; this is clearly a nonsensical story, probably first orated by someone after having several pints in the White Horse, especially since the Emperors have no legs – mind you, enough students manage to end up there legless.

The Emperors are routinely referred to by students as The Twelve Apostles; however, these are evidently not mathematical students since there are actually thirteen of them!

A complete lack of any existing evidence rarely curtails active speculation, and this remains the case with the Emperors – one figure is sometimes considered to be Bacchus the Roman god of wine, which would chime consistently with most students' value system. And with tedious regularity, traffic cones appear as Emperor's hats.

Anthony Gormley statue suitably attired by Exeter students for Burns Night.

Emperors' Heads outside the Sheldonian Theatre.

RECORD HIGH

Oxford students have always forged a sporting reputation, ranging from historical accomplishments (Roger Bannister's sub-four-minute mile at the Iffley Road track) to varsity tiddlywinks. Many accomplish sporting excellence in Oxford, and some even achieve world records.

As a child, did you ever dream of appearing on Roy Castle's *Record Breakers*? No? Maybe one Oxford student did. Hosting twin dreams of one day gaining public admiration and respect for holding a *bona fide* record, whilst simultaneously winning a place at Oxford: the world's foremost University (get over it, Cambridge) providing didactic excellence coupled with an irresistible inspiration to pursue knowledge and academic achievement.

Whereas most of us willingly grab a few extra minutes cocooned in duvet heat following the quotidian torture of the alarm clock, this Oxford undergraduate rose at dawn to commence training for his goal – such uncompromising dedication exposing a true champion's mentality.

Like most record breakers, he disciplined himself to a strict non-deviating dietary intake (mainly salt water and supermarket own-brand cider). His hard work was duly rewarded, for he accomplished the record of throwing up in each of Oxford's thirty-eight Colleges. I know, that's just sick.

A LEVEL PLAYING FIELD

News broke in 2010 that Lady Margaret Hall had sent down a student after discovering he had fraudulently obtained an Oxford place by falsifying his academic record, forging school documents to show that he had obtained thirteen A levels at A grade. With hindsight, thirteen A levels at A grade was a suspiciously implausible claim. As were the accompanying achievements probably also listed in the teenager's CV: 4 Nobel prizes, 2 BAFTA Lifetime Achievement Awards, 1966 World Cup winner's medal, landed on moon five months before Neil Armstrong, discovered America, invented wood.

PRESIDENT TEDDY RULES A VOTE
(hint, you need to say it quickly)

Queen's JCR reacted to alleged political interference from the authorities by declaring that a candidate standing for forthcoming election to the post of JCR President in 2009/10 would be Mr

Clumsy Teddy. Voters were not put off by predictable smear stories – presumably planted by rival candidates – claiming that he was a stuffed bear. Being caught regularly sleeping with his mistress also failed to cause political fur to fly.

At a time when voters unanimously conformed to an orthodoxy that politicians were mendacious and untrustworthy, Clumsy Teddy arrived to prove that not all bears made a mess in the woods. Just as some had once feared America wasn't yet sufficiently progressive and courageous to elect a black man as President, supporters similarly feared that being a teddy bear would put off unenlightened voters in

Mr Clumsy Teddy. (Photo courtesy of Lizzie Burrowes)

some states (being students, these would be the key states of undress, drunkenness and agitation). But this was one electoral college system that would pick the right candidate.

In what became a fiercely fought campaign, Clumsy got his claws into the opposition. But whereas the other candidates offered little deviation from the norm, Teddy was able to show that not everyone enters politics just to get their snout in the trough/honey pot/salmon river. And so he was elected with a huge 51 per cent mandate from the voters, ensuring Teddy bears responsibility for Queen's JCR.

Clumsy Teddy's handler, Lizzie Burrowes, informed the *Oxford Student*: 'Having owned the bear since the age of one I can tell you that Clumsy Teddy doesn't tell lies, doesn't claim expenses and he has only slept in one bed – unlike many of Britain's politicians.'

ABOUT THE AUTHOR

Richard O. Smith is a previous winner of the National Football Writer of the Year Award, having written and edited the award-winning football fanzine *From Behind Your Fences*. He has also written for the *Independent*, *Guardian* and *When Saturday Comes* and has contributed aired material to various comedians and BBC Radio 4 shows, including *The News Quiz*, *Now Show* and *Heresy*.

He conducts the Eccentric Oxford Walking Tour (during which he generally insults Cambridge for a living). Details of the tour can be found at http://www.oxfordwalks.co.uk, as can the contact details for booking a private tour. Participants should dress for an entertaining walking tour packed with intriguing facts mined from Oxford's history (decent weather not included). The tour includes reference to some of Oxford's scientists, novelists, Prime Ministers, actors, pioneers, poets, television stars, criminals and politicians (there is some inevitable cross-over within the last two categories).

He also has a Twitter homepage http://twitter.com/RichardOSmith1 where further details of his latest projects and publications can be found.

Richard lives in Oxford with his wife Catherine.

BIBLIOGRAPHY

Risking prolixity with its 8,000 pages *The History of the University of Oxford* edited by Brook, M.G. and Curthoys M. C. (Clarendon, 1994) weighs in at a potential bookshelf buckling eight hardback volumes, yet is highly recommended for any discerning scholar intent on knowing not only what major figures in the University's creation and history had for breakfast, but whether their bacon was smoked or unsmoked Thorough to the extent of being downright intimidating – although the gpp (gags per page) ratio is unsurprisingly low. Other useful books include:

Acland, Henry *The Oxford Museum* (1893)

Adams, Pauline *Somerville for Women* (OUP, 1996)

Barr, W.G. *Exeter College* (Exeter, 2000)

Breen, Richard and Mudannayake, Suresh *Oxford Odd Fellows and Funny Tales* (Penny, 1977)

Green, V.H.H. *History of Oxford University* (1974)

Hibbert, Christopher & Edward *Encyclopaedia of Oxford* (MacMillan, 1988)

Hopkins, Clare *Trinity: 450 Years of an Oxford College Community* (OUP, 2005)

Jebb, Miles *Colleges of Oxford* (Constable, 1992)

Jo & Hayley *Our Oxford* (Capture Oxford Moment, 2006)

Johnson, Rachel *The Oxford Myth* (Weidenfeld Nicolson, 1988)

Jones, John, *Balliol College A History* (OUP, 1997)

Kelly, J.N.D. *St Edmund Hall* (1989, OUP)

le Vay, Benedict *Eccentric Oxford* (Bradt, 2004)

Martin, G.H. & Highfield, J.R.L. *History of Merton College* (OUP, 1997)